SOMEBODY UP THERE
LIKES
ME
TOO

A MEMOIR
BY GEORGE FITZGERALD

EDITED AND
WITH AN INTRODUCTION
BY JASON O'TOOLE

This book is a true story.
Some names and places have been changed to protect innocent parties.

First published by Watchman Publications 2005

Cover Design and layout: Agnieszka O'Toole
        email: dubliner15@yahoo.com
Cover Photography: Jason O'Toole
        email: jmotoole@iol.ie
Proof read by: PJ Flanagan of Scriptext
        email: scriptext@eircom.net

ISBN: 0-9549883-0-2

POBOX 27, Bray, Co. Wicklow, Ireland
Email: somebodyuptherelikesme2@hotmail.com

Acknowledgments

First and foremost, I would like to thank the God and Father of the Lord Jesus Christ for his grace mercy and love towards me. This one's for you Lord.

I would also like to thank Sandra my beautiful wife, for the last twenty three years. And a special thanks for the last twenty months, while she became Mother, Father, and Brother to me, Daniel and Nathan while I committed myself to work on this manuscript. To Daniel Jonathan, and Nathan Lewis Fitzgerald, my sons, I'm proud of yis... thanks. To My Mother and Father, George and Marie Fitzgerald for all the years, thanks.To my brothers Joseph Wesley and Pat. To Peter Traynor who skillfully and prayerfully guided me to my destination, thanks Peter. To PJ Flanagan, for his persistence in helping me develop my technique. To Neville Thomson for helping me see the bigger picture, thanks Nev. To Barry and Duggy, my faithful friends. To Jayne and Pat Burns - thanks for all your help. Thanks to Rosemary Whelan for all her encouragement.Thanks to John Burns for all his help with the advertisement of this book. To Jimmy and Yvonne for your friendship. Thanks to all at St Mark's. To Ken O'Brien, for his friendship throughout the years. To the best doctor in the world, Dr Ekky, for seeing me through the toughest time of my life... thanks doctor. Vincent Gannon and Simon for fixing the computer. And to all my in-laws and family whose names are too vast to mention - thanks. With all boxers and all musicians, there is always a great manager standing in the background writers are no exception. None of this work would have been complete without the help of Jason O'Toole. Also thanks to Agnieszka for her work on designing the cover.

Thank you...

"This story is not mine alone...it's yours or it's your brothers, maybe it's your father's. Who am I? A man who went for a walk. What did I see? Beautiful flowers, the tallest mountains and the clearest blue streams. All this set against the backdrop of shark-infested waters, star-filled skies and beams of light that come from the early morning sun."

- George Fitzgerald.

INTRODUCTION

It is an extremely difficult - and sometimes painful - experience to write an autobiography. The writer who undertakes such an unenviable task must revisit his past in an analytic method in order to be true to himself and the reader. It can be an emotionally thorny experience to conjure up and mull over the past; this is particularly true if the writer decides to be openly honest and discuss painful (perhaps even still hurtful) memories.

George Fitzgerald has undertaken the difficult task of penning a refreshingly ingenuous account of his life. This book is a quintessential story of a working-class Dubliner with aspirations to break out of his restrictive (both spiritual and financial) existence and achieve success and celebrity status. Before the birth of the so-called 'Celtic Tiger', Dublin was a city populated with limited possibilities for working-class teenagers who could not afford - nor muster up enthusiasm for - a third-level education. The opportunity to procure a 'career' (rather than an uninspiring apprenticeship or factory tiling) was also tenuously improbable.

The only other option open to the likes of George was to discover and develop sporting or artistic talents. The northside of Dublin - particularly Ballymun and Finglas (where George grew-up) - was a hotbed for such talent. It is no exaggeration to suggest that a substantial percentage of Ireland's latter day 'heroes' are from the northside of the Liffey. The easiest example is U2, with Bono and the lyrically brilliant Gavin Friday (of the Virgin Prunes) growing up in the same community (and at the same time) as George. Others include the popular band Aslan, the authors Roddy Doyle and Dermot Bolger, and the actors Colm Meaney (of Star Trek fame) and Brendan O'Carroll. The sporting heroes from this area is equally impressive: Ronnie Whelan from Finglas was one of the most talented soccer players to ply his trade in England when he captained Liverpool (and Ireland on occasion) ; while even one of the famous Matt Busby babes was from Cabra ("a stones throw from Finglas").

The prospect of a number one hit single, or starring in an Hollywood blockbuster, or even scoring the winning goal in a FA Cup final, seemed a reachable goal for many working class dreamers. Unfortunately the majority of George's contemporaries with such dreams of fame eventually discovered they were embracing illusions of grandeur or, in unfortunate cases, untimely in their endeavours to reach the big time.

Unlike many others, George was fortunately able to fulfil his quest for glory. He was blessed with a build and an athletic intelligence to surpass even his own wildest expectations in the boxing ring. Unfortunately, he would discover he did not have the stomach to fulfil his potential; it was a case of homesickness and lovesickness that made George retire from the sport which promised him the possibility of money and fame.

His hunger for success soon manifested itself again when he formed the very popular band, The D-11 Runners. It was an apt name because the band were indeed running away from something - they were attempting to run away from a life of mundane jobs or unemployment. It was a dream come true for George; for he was achieving top ten hits in a band which included his brothers and his soon-to-be-wife. Sadly, unforeseen circumstances, which you will read about in George's 'hard hitting' autobiography, basically destroyed the band. The D-11 Runners were 'The Commitments' before Roddy Doyle wrote his novella.

Fast forward fifteen years, George is working as a car park attendant. It would have been easier for him to have not told this story. After all, nobody likes failure. But this is not a story about failure -

it is a story about discovering the 'inner success'.

At the start of this introduction, I stated that it was a difficult experience to write an honest autobiography. After reading this book, most readers will agree that George was openly candid in this book. He wrote frankly about his desires, the deaths of several childhood friends, and ultimately the failures of his magnificent successes. He even wrote about the poignant experience of losing a child. During the past two years, George jostled daily with these inner demons as he attempt to put down on paper his life experiences. For that alone, I doff my hat to George. He has written a honest and compelling life story.

As an interesting after note, George paid a visit to my home a few weeks before his book was due to print. We went up to my office and George (perhaps instinctively) picked up an old magazine I was editor of and flicked it open to an article I had written about TS O'Rourke, an Irish author who has written several successful crime books. In the article, O'Rourke put emphasis on the need to write about your own experiences.

George laughed for several minutes. Eventually, he said: "You are not going to believe this, but this article inspired me to write my autobiography. When Trevor explained about writing about your own experiences, he gave me the confidence to write my life story. I can't believe it was you who wrote this article which inspired me."

"Perhaps it was destiny," I replied.

"It was more than destiny…it was God's hand," George said.

- Jason O'Toole, March 2005

*This book is dedicated to
the memory of
Harry McGowan,
Paul and Paddy Kearney,
and also the great
Packie Stafford*

ROUND 1

The little boy watched the fight from behind a huge rock that was covered by the shadow of the trees. The swords clashed, the man in the green suit jumped back. It was a fence to the death. Then, Robin Hood, our hero, charged back into the duel, holding onto his smile in the face of great danger. Suddenly a brilliant light burst upon them, blinding the dark King, while our hero sprung into the air, pinning him to a tree. Little John arrived on a big black horse and picked up the boy. Meanwhile Robin Hood stripped the king of all his clothes and they all rode off into the sunset.

Joseph, my twin brother, and I sat on the floor clapping when our hero saved the day. We stayed there until the black and white picture was reduced to a dot.

"Ok boys it's time for bed," ma called.

We rose off the floor and walked down the hall holding our da's hand.

"Good night boys, say your prayers," ma shouted.

"Ok Ma," we shouted in unison.

"Da will yah tell me a s-nory?" I chanced while he tucked me in.

"Ok but it's going to be a short one. Are yah ready?"

"Once upon a time in a faraway land there was a little boy."

I smiled and rubbed my feet together when I heard 'little boy'. I glance over at Joseph - he was fast asleep.

"Da," I said cutting in on his story, "when I gets to be a big boy, I'm going to learn all snorys and tell all boys snorys."

"That's a good boy. But it's story George," da urged.

"Snorys."

"Very good," he replied and before he could say another word I was fast asleep.

An angry wind blew fiercely at the bedroom window just above my bed. The shifting curtains brushed my face, as a peel of thunder ripped through the night sky. I shot up and just as quickly dived back under the blankets. I lifted my head and stared at the walls, imagining that they were closing in on me. The thunder raged across the blackened sky, forcefully shaking the window. I drew a long breath and disappeared under the blankets again, covering my chin so that my eyes could only be seen.

It was the dead of night. The streets below were silent. Where was Robin Hood? Would he make an appearance? I waited and waited, but he didn't come. Once again I directed my eyes towards the ceiling. My lip quivered.

The dark shadows grew from a creeping hand into a hideous monster. The roar of thunder terrified me. Somehow I managed to fling back the blankets, flee past my sleeping brother, and reach the top of the hallway.

The walls began to move, bringing me face to face with the bodiless Indian men hanging above me. I swallowed hard, fell into a crawling position, and stole past them. My body still trembling as they seemed to watch my every move. My ears became attracted to the voice coming from the television as if it was a friend.

I reached for the handle. The door opened and on seeing da sitting on his chair, I flew straight onto his lap. I was still shuddering when ma brought me a little drink and wiped my cheeks.

"Yah don't have to be afraid," she said, as she ran her fingers through my hair.

Resting in da's strong arms and with ma's reassurance, I finally felt safe.

"I can count to twenty," I muttered into da's face.

"I know yah can son," he said, rubbing my head.

My eyes closed and I was taken away into the world of fairy-tale adventures and childish dreams.

When the morning came I was back in bed, just lying there counting numbers in my head and talking to God and his angels the way the teacher told us. She said that God and his angels always listen to boys that tell them things. So I told him about my little brother and how he spits out his food when he doesn't like it. And then I told him about scary monsters and how Robin Hood never turns up.

The thoughts of the night rushed through my mind, the darkness, the stillness of the room and the monster trying to eat me. I turned my head into the pillow and prayed to God to save me from monsters that eat you at night. Then I looked up at the ceiling and said: "I can count to twenty."

The sound of flapping wings landing on the balcony woke my brother. He jumped up and yawned, and when the yawning was over he leapt out of bed and pulled back the curtains.

"Joseph..." I said, taking my eyes off the black sky for a moment. "Aliens took me away last night, when I was asleep."

"I know, I was there too," he replied, nodding his head.

"Were you really?" I gasped with excitement, waiting to hear his version of events.

"Yeah, I went up a hill and it was brilliant. There were loads of sweets and big teddy bears everywhere."

I pulled my knees tightly to my chest, pulling the blankets up to my mouth, and hung on to his every word. He was padding around the room expanding on his adventure with the visitors from the moon, when I cut him off:

"I went up the hill as well, there was a big castle that had a big load of trees outside and the trees had big, big eyes, and two mouths."

Joseph stopped in his tracks and sat on the bed when he heard about the big eyes and two mouths.

"What happened next?"

"I crept inside a big door and saw a ghost who I was sure was an alien. He said hello to me but I didn't say hello back. I just kept running and running 'till I fell off a mountain top and then I woke up."

Everything went quiet in the little bedroom. Joseph suddenly jumped up and went screaming, "Ma, Ma, George is frightening me."

The door slammed loudly, causing me to jump out of the bed. Now I was running, screaming behind him, pulling the long blanket between the streaks of light coming in from the sitting room window.

The first person I saw when I entered the kitchen was Pat, our little brother. He was strapped into his chair firing food around the place. Ma was washing dishes. Da was in the bathroom shaving and we could hear him sing. So I pushed Joseph out of the way and jumped onto my favourite stool.

The kitchen had a small window with lace curtains, and tiny vases, filled with smelling flowers. Ma said that she would close her eyes and imagine she was standing in a beautiful garden. Da said it was good that she imagined it because on the tenth floor there wasn't much hope of a garden! I would close my eyes and pretend I was in the Doctor Who box. But da said, "There's no point in being boastful, the kitchen's not that big!"

Our family had moved here in 1967, to the land of dreams, the new world of the working class. For tenants it was comfortable but outsiders would see it in an altogether different light. The massive tower blocks housed some eighty families each. Seven towers in all, built in grey concrete, surrounded by four storey and eight storey blocks. It was the corporation's monuments to the housing problem of the early sixties.

It was now May 1970. The old radio started playing a song called '*Where's your mama gone?*' Joseph and I joined in while Pat played with his spoon, sending more food across the kitchen. We could hear da whistling as he walked down the hall from the bathroom.

"Right boys wash your hands, face and teeth. Yah can't have any breakfast before your holy communion; afterwards yah can have a big treat."

"This is your big day, a wonderful day," ma said with a smile.

By nine-thirty we were all dressed and ready to go. Joseph and I left the flat and raced across the landing. We pressed the button on the lift. It went red which meant it was working. We were glad about that. Da had said he was going to the shop but he would meet us downstairs. Ma arrived with Pat in his buggy and, as if by magic, the door opened.

Ma wore a very smart blue suit and a big hat while da wore a grey silver type suit and black shoes. He carried a raincoat draped over his arm. Joseph and I were dressed in school blazers, short trousers and long white stockings. We even had the same black slip-on shoes and school caps that carried the logo.

There was a glint of pride in our parents eyes and we felt like we were real little boys now.

"Ah, they look smashing Marie," a neighbour hollered from an open window on the second floor. Ma turned and waved.

"There's a few shillings for the boys," said the same voice, as we watched coins fall and land on the path as if from heaven. Joseph and I sprinted in different directions, while ma tried to draw us back.

"Come on," da said as we divided the money and crammed it into our pockets, discussing what sweets we might buy later.

"Thanks. We'll see yah later Mary," ma said, waving back as we moved on.

"She won't see me later," I heard da say, through the side of his mouth.

♪

We arrived at the church, walked down the aisle and found a seat. That wasn't hard - we were the first to arrive! The benches must have been just cleaned because the smell of polish was still very strong. The sun was now streaming through the coloured glass. It was like the whole world was on fire outside and we were safe like Noah and his family inside the ark.

At the top of the church a chubby-faced boy dressed in a long white dress was standing with his elbows on top of the cushioned chairs. He jerked his head back and gave a little sigh that said he was bored, before sitting down, fixing his gaze on us.

"I met May O' Rourke in town last week," ma said.

"Yeah and how's she keeping?" asked da.

"Well, she's away from Tommy and back living in her mammy's, there was terrible trouble I heard."

Da looked at ma, ma looked at da, and they both looked at us, and we looked at them, while the boy in the dress stared at us all. So I looked towards Jesus, whose eyes seemed very sad.

I let my mind drift and thought of Susan that lived in number twenty in our block. Last week she was in her kitchen and I was there too. She went to the press, took out the bread and jam, and gave some to her little brother who said, "Ta-ta."

"Georgie Fitzgerald, would yah like bread and jam?"

"No thanks, me ma said I should never take anything from strangers."

"Well, my ma said yah should give nice things to strangers."

While we stood there, I wondered which one of us was the

stranger? I thought about how nice it would be to kiss her. But then the teacher's words about sin came rattling back and I knew for sure that my soul was dammed to hell for having such thoughts in a holy place.

The priest made his way towards us. I bowed my head in prayer. He bent down to talk with da who lifted his ear to listen to him. And ma smiled, nodding in agreement.

Big people always smile and nod when they meet holy people. They nod their heads, their chins, their hands, and if the person is really holy, they give a little nod with their knees. Like the way they do when they approach the altar. And then they sit back down until another holy person comes along and the smiling and nodding starts all over again, until the old people who sit at the back are fast asleep from all the nodding.

Suddenly the large timber doors opened and the creaking sound sent an echo through the entire church. Families rushed in, pushing each other out of the way to get a seat.

The bell rang. Everyone stood up and leaned forward. Then they knelt and they sat back down again. When the bell rang the second time everyone stood up again. The parents stood back while we stood out in two single rows, our hands tightly pressed together. All the boys were dressed in uniforms while all the girls were dressed like princesses.

We watched the priest reading from the big word. My heart clung to me because I knew what happened next. I was handed the little wafer that had Jesus inside, and I swallowed it.

For us boys this was a big day, we received Jesus. Well that's what the priest told us, so now we were holy. The bell rang again and we blessed our faces and left all holy, running around with Jesus inside.

Once we were outside, I ran along the grey concrete steps situated at the side of the school. I rested, tilting my head back underneath the summer sun that had made an immense appearance on our holy day. Life was new to me like all young boys. The air was clear, everything was fresh. It was a giant adventure, but like all adventures real or imaginary, there are always dark passages lying ahead. Nobody gets to rest in the harvest of his dreams without first entering into to the dungeons of his nightmares.

For this little boy one lay just ahead.

The woman, who sat on a chair in front of the butcher's shop, was portly with large shoulders and big jolly cheeks. She had all the airs and graces of a grandmother, even though her appearance was slightly haggard.

"Ah there yis are," she said, pulling herself from the seat as we approached the shop. But before she did, she took a sup from a little bottle and then buried it in her smock.

"Ah would yah look at the twins, Marie. They're getting so big, as big as trees," she beamed while shading her eyes, surveying us again from head to toe. "As big as trees, I'm not codden yah."

"It doesn't matter how big they get as long as they behave themselves," ma replied.

I got the impression ma was mildly disagreeing with the old lady. So I stole a glance at my reflection in the window and wondered what trees she was talking about.

"It must be the ones that ma grows in her kitchen," Joseph said, and both of us laughed into our hands.

"Now, what can I get yah love?" the lady asked.

"A ring of white pudding, a half pound of sausages, and six lean rashers. Oh and a half dozen eggs," ma replied.

"Is George in work?" enquired the old lady as she wheeled away from the counter.

"Yeah, but he'll be home early today. He got a new job over in Glasnevin."

"Ah that's great," she replied, standing with her back to us.

I jumped up on the counter and watched her take the last sup from the bottle, when she thought nobody was looking. Then she whisked any crumbs that had rested on her smock, wrapped the food, wiped her lips, and blew both of us a kiss.

"There's a lovely bit of pudding. I know what's good for boys with all that growing in them," she said.

"She knows what's good for herself as well," I confided to Joseph, both of us laughing again while we waited for our lolly-pops.

"There yis go boys," she said, handing us the lollypops.

"What do yis say?" ma said.

"Thanks," we said happily and off we marched out of the shop.

A blue sky hung over our heads, its blistering rays blessing the whole neighbourhood. The heat became more intense, blanketing the little balcony where we sat in our white shorts bare-footed, still licking our lollypops. Inside, breakfast was being prepared. Plates of food were being placed on the table; eggs, bacon, sausages, and toast. The glass door with the narrow frame opened. It was da.

"Right boys, your breakfast is nearly ready," he said, as he stood for a moment smoking his cigarette.

His jet black hair shone in the sunlight. I looked at him gazing over the balcony. He smiled down on us. We smiled back. Da was a tall figure of a man who all his life carried the appearance of a movie star. He was warm-hearted, kind, and of good character. Always our hero, we loved him very much as we did our mother, a small attractive woman who always had room for a laugh. If there was anything funny to be found, our mother would find it.

As we rested in the harbour of our childish dreams, a voice from the neighbouring balcony interrupted us: "Did yeah make a million yesterday, boys?"

"Never yah mind Annie," our da answered with a gentle laugh.

"Go way out of that, Georgie. Ah they're good boys," she remarked.

The lace curtain that hung along the door moved. Da switched his glance and noticed little Pat behind it. He picked him up and held him in the air calling him funny names, the names big people call babies.

Ma called us from the kitchen and we all went in for breakfast.

"Mary was here. She asked if she could see the twins dressed in their new clothes," ma said to da, who threw his eyes towards the ceiling and nodded a silent yes.

From the time we were born, people would stop my ma and ask if they could look at the twins in the pram. Twins are born into a world of attention, a place of gazing eyes, and a bond of unity where identity and individuality are lost.

"What's it like to be a twin?"

That's the golden question we have been asked all our lives.

"Well what's it like not to be one?"

What I can tell you is that you feel special because wherever you go, you're the centre of attraction. The downside is that everyone who walks into your world seems to carelessly take on the role as judge and jury in the comparison game.

"He's like his da or he's like his ma."

"Who's the clever one?"

"Who the thick one?"

"He's the taller, the smaller, or the fatter."

But the upside is you've always got someone to watch your back and the word 'loneliness' is only a word that appears in the dictionary because from the moment of conception you have a companion.

♪

The summer months were over and soon it was back to school. September passed. And October arrived. It was Halloween time.

This was a special day.

I entered the classroom to the sound of chairs being rattled. I moved quickly to my seat. We were being told ghost stories today. That's what the teacher said. And she was right because we were no sooner at our tables when she began telling us about Quasimodo, the man with the hunch back. She told us to stand up, and after she finished telling us that story, she told us a story, all about creeping monsters.

I felt like crying but I couldn't because the boys would call me names, like mammy's boy or sissy. So I stuck my fingers in my ears and counted lambs jumping over fences in my head.

Before she finished, the door opened and in walked the Reverend Mother.

"Be seated boys, the Reverend Mother would like to talk to you for a moment."

"Hello boys," the Reverend Mother said looking over the rim of her glasses.

We never answered. We were too afraid in case we said the wrong thing and that would leave our souls damned in hell. After a moment of silence she spoke again.

"Well boys, as you are well aware Christmas is not too far off, so what I've done is brought in this box that I will leave here in the front of the class. And what I want you to do is to put in a penny a week for the poor little black babies that live in Africa."

Nobody said a word and I wondered how the black babies who lived in Africa could get the money if it was on our table. She continued to tell us about the poor little black babies.

I thought about the little baby that they called Rockabye Baby, the one that fell out of the tree. He must have been a poor black baby because I never saw a baby sleeping in a tree. I whispered this to little Johnny who sat beside me. He said he saw a black baby stuck in a tree across from his block. He said that it was so far up in the tree that the fire brigade had to come and get him down. Fat Billy, who sat behind us chuckled.

"That was a cat, Johnny, yah thick."

Poor Johnny's face lit up like a Christmas tree. He was so embarrassed. It wasn't the first time I saw Johnny go all red. Last week he went to the toilet all down his leg and left a big puddle on the floor. The teacher told us to fold our arms and go to sleep. But I couldn't because of the smell. Fat Billy said it smelt like cats. I said I never smelt a cat, so I wouldn't know if it did or not.

After the Reverend Mother was finished talking, she left the room, leaving behind a large box of sweets for us boys. The teacher put her books down and handed them out one at a time. Just as she was about to sit down, I walked up to the top of the class and spat mine out. It sounded like popcorn popping when it hit the bottom of the bin right beside the desk.

Miss O'Brien screamed my name. I froze. She pulled me towards her with a ferocious jerk and rushed me screaming towards the corner. My feet went from walking to running as I tried to keep up with the long strides she took.

The corner was dark and lonely. I could smell the disinfectant from the floor and sense laughing eyes hiding behind tiny hands. There was no yellow brick road here.

"Go to sleep," the teacher cried to the boys, and in one quick movement she turned her head back towards me.

"So you don't like that sweet," she screamed again.

"No," I replied.

"Ungrateful, ungrateful. God hates ungratefulness," she yelled.

She walked to the top of the class and when she returned she had a hat in her hand. It was pointy with the word "dunce" written on it. She cowered over me like a shadow.

"Stand up," she cried and when I did she crowned me with the pointy hat. Moving forward 'till our faces nearly touched, she exclaimed: "You're a dunce."

"Will I be a dunce forever, Miss?" She paused and stared at me. "Yes, forever," she finally snapped.

I fell to the floor and shrank into the corner. The teacher lifted me with one hand and marched me back to my seat. I stared out the window and watched the autumn leaves fall, wondering if ma knew how long forever was.

ROUND 2

"*Christmas is coming, the goose is getting fat, please put a penny in the old man's hat. If yah haven't got a penny, a ha-penny will do, if yah haven't got a ha-penny, God help you.*"

It was the song that Fat Billy, Joe and I sang as we skipped in front of ma and Pat a few days before Christmas. Fat Billy rolled up his sleeves and ran towards the shops. And when he got there, he pressed his nose against the window so much that he reminded me of the man the teacher told us about, Quasimodo.

"Look! It's baby Jesus and cows. And there's the tu-tu train Santy's bringing me."

"Ma, can we look at the baby Jesus, can we, Ma?"

"Ok, ok, but only for a few minutes, we've got to get home. Your dad's putting up the Christmas tree."

So off we went with Pat shouting, "Baaa-bby dusus."

"There's the baby Jesus, his mammy and his letting-on daddy," Billy said, pointing to each one, his nose still pressed against the window.

"Oh I'm telling on you, you said a curse. Ma, Billy said a curse."

"He did Ma," Joe added.

Ma threw us a look, the ones big people have when they feel sad.

"Stop telling tales boys, Santy's watching, remember."

Then she turned and had a conversation with a shopkeeper.

A man emerged out of one of the shops. He walked along the street with his hat cocked back, his coat swinging wildly, and his right hand buried in his pocket.

His first words were addressed to ma courteously, the next ones addressed to his son harshly.

"Right Billy, come on it's time to go home."

"But Da, look! There's the tu-tu Santy's bringing me," he said with his face still stuck to the window.

"Yeah, ask him to bring me one as well. Come on let's go."

"Ok Da," he sighed and off they went. Billy didn't hold his da's hand but he did turn and wave.

"Right boys, let's finish getting the rest of the messages," ma said. We did and when we were done we headed back to the flat.

"Wow! Look at that," Joe shouted when we walked in the door. It's the biggest tree in the world."

"Yeah, it's even the biggest in Ballymun," I said, shouting over the radio that had started singing again.

Da loved the song, so he left the tree and started dancing with ma. She was laughing and she laughed more when Joseph and I joined in as Pat clapped and bounced up and down in his pram.

When da went back to the tree he called us over. He told us he had cut down the tree all by himself. On the way home he had fought off two big bears and then ran all the way home with the biggest tree in the world.

Joe and I stood there with our mouths open, eyes growing larger and just when we were about to cry, he grabbed us and tiddled us. He told us that he was only joking, it was only one bear!

I felt very happy because Santy was coming and it was Jesus' birthday. Then I thought about Billy and his da. And I felt sad. I went into the bedroom and asked God and his angels to tell

Santy to bring Billy's da a tu-tu.

A week passed and Christmas Eve arrived. After our bath we put on our new pyjamas - the ones me Auntie May got us - and we gave ma a kiss, da a kiss, Pat a kiss and each other a kiss. We went to bed and talked about toys and sweets and we marked the second last X on the calendar.

Later I got out of bed and stared out the window to see if I could see Santy coming. I didn't, but I did see the stars. I pressed my hands together, wished Jesus the happiest birthday ever and jumped back into bed.

Christmas morning finally arrived and there were no more Xs left to mark on the calendar. Joseph woke me tugging at my blankets. "George. George, Santy been here," he cried, his voice full of excitement.

My heart jumped for joy when I remembered what day it was. We stood in silence for a moment then the silence broke into a shrill of excitement.

Joseph was the first to walk out of the room. He looked back at me and suddenly both of us raced along the hallway. We reached the sittingroom door. Joseph opened it ever so gently and peeked in. Our little eyes could hardly take in what they were seeing. There were boxes of toys neatly stacked. Along the ground were annuals, the Dandy and Beano, resting on selection boxes. In that moment, a memory was captured that was framed forever in our minds. We stood there with our mouths opened and hearts filled with the most incredible feeling.

In the background we could hear da getting up. We heard the shuffling of his feet coming down the hall as we went about opening presents like men who had found hidden treasure.

"Happy Christmas boys," da said.

"Happy Christmas Da. Look what Santy left us!"

"Well you must have been good boys," he added sitting, in his armchair.

Just then ma arrived with Pat dangling in her arms.

"Oh my Lord, look what Santa brought. Look George, he must have been hungry because all the pudding is gone."

Ma helped Pat crawl through the rubble of boxes guiding him to his appointed destination.

The lights on the Christmas tree lit up the room. Songs were playing on the radio as we unravelled the boxes. The atmosphere was electric. Suddenly ma asked us a question:

"George, Joseph, what are in those two boxes over there?"

It was our bikes. We had been so excited that we totally forgot about the very thing we had asked for. That Christmas we spent in 64 Eamonn Ceannt Tower, Ballymun, is a time we look back on with great fondness.

ROUND 3

It's a Saturday afternoon and the summer had arrived. The year is 1973.

There is a boy, he's young, walking through the streets listening to American music coming from a radio on the balcony of one of the flats. He steps out from the crib, rolls his shoulders back, places his hand over his mouth and roars. His cry is like that of a vendor. He walks in and out between the sun and the shadows, takes deep drags on his cigarette, and flicks it away. When he doesn't receive any answer he moves off.

I pulled up the window, stared down at the boy as he walked across the playground which was crowded with children. I closed the window and left the flat. The lift was jammed, so I took the stairs. There was mud on the steps and writing on the walls; the air was strong with the smell of urine that wafted up from the basement.

Men and women stood with prams that were filled with screaming babies, their voices echoing throughout the block. I avoided them, and the mucky steps, by moving with skilful ease gained from avoiding mucky stairs and crying babies!

Outside on the streets the older boys, who wore tweed caps and had cigarettes hanging from their mouths, played more adult games. They would stand a few feet away from the wall in a squatting position, tossing coins. Barney, an older man who lived on our block, stood in the middle of the boys who were now having a row over the coins.

"Little Georgie, will yah bring those cigarettes over to Mrs Murphy?" he said, pointing towards the woman standing at the other block.

He had a deep plump voice that matched his red cheeks and his jumper reminded me of Val Doonican.

"Would yah like a cigarette Mick?" Barney said to his friend.

"Not a puff, not a puff," said Mick waving his hand in the air.

"Here, have a smoke will yah," Barney then said, noticing that Mick's voice said one thing but his eye said something else.

"Ah go on then," he muttered, winking at me.

"Right son off yah go, sure ye'll be there before yer back. And when yah get back I'll have a little reward for yah."

So off I ran with the cigarettes in hand and the reward on my mind.

Mrs Murphy was standing with her arms folded talking to another woman. They were middle-aged, portly women with scarves tightly pressed on their heads - even in the hot sun.

"Goodness gracious, Miss Fay," Mrs Murphy said, thrusting her head back and staring up towards a window.

"Do yah know what he's up to now?" Mrs Murphy said, tapping Mrs Fay's arm.

"I saw him earlier over in the shops. He's up to no good let me tell yah."

"He was wailing up at that flat this morning," Mrs Murphy added.

"He was probably looking for a sponge, for his sore arse his da gave 'em," Miss Fay replied with a heavy sigh.

After standing there for what seemed like a lifetime, I began pulling at the woman's coat calling her name.

"Mrs Murphy ! Mrs Murphy !"

She drew back with an air of surprise but her face glowed

when she caught sight of the smokes.

"Ah thanks love, you're a star, here's ten pence for your trouble," she said, rubbing my head.

I heard screaming coming from the streets. I stabbed my head over the wall and saw a woman crying frantically. To her right a youth was running in and out between the passing cars with a handbag in his hand. It was the boy who stood at the bottom of our block earlier.

He weaved in and out between the crowds, passing cars, and a line of workmen on the side of the street. Shouts came from the shops, the flats, and the men who worked there. Some of them chased after him with hammers in their hands. A gang of men stood in front of the shaven-headed boy, trying to block him. But he widened the gap by bursting through a maze of angry faces.

I shrunk down at the garage wall, watching him race across the grass and reach the place where I was cowered. His face was red and he breathed heavily, making funny movements with his mouth. I tried to move but he riveted his eyes on me, like a rabbit in a snare.

I could hear the rustling of feet, the cries from the nearing crowd and the police siren ringing in the distance. Just as he was about to strike me, I sprang to my feet, darted across the open spaces with a little voice in my head saying: Run, Georgie, run.

The police cars drew nearer. A cold sweat broke over me. I looked towards our block. A stream of people were lining the windows and balconies. The doors of the police car slammed as the Gardai jumped out. I threw a glance over my shoulder and saw that the thief was doing the same thing. Another police car screeched to a halt. But the boy disappeared into the basement of the flats.

I raced back up the stairwells, ran past the boys playing hide and go seek and girls singing Beatles' songs until I reached the second floor. I met Fat Billy. He was standing with his back against the wall. He called to me: "It's me birthday today George. I'm eight - same age as you now."

"Happy birthday, Billy," I said trying to catch my breath.

The smell of cabbage floated along the hallway. Cardboard boxes that had been flattened stretched across the floor. I picked up an old radio that was lying in the corner. Billy said his granda had won it in the war for being a hero.

"I didn't know that yah could win radios for being a hero, Billy."

"Yeah, yah can, but only when they run out of medals. They must have always been running out of medals because me granda has about ten thousand radios."

"Really?"

"Yeah really, if yah want I'll ask him can I give yah one, cause I think he's getting another five next week and then he'll have twenty thousand."

"Wow, a real hero," I said in wonderment.

"Yep, and I'm going to be a hero some day. That's what me granda says."

Billy's ma peeped her head out of the bedroom.

"Come on, time to come in Billy. That boy's mammy will be looking for him, tell him to go home."

She didn't have to repeat herself, I just ran without saying goodbye to Billy.

When I reached our landing, Joseph, Peter and John were playing hide and go seek.

"George, I'm telling on you."

He rushed in towards ma and da who were sitting at the kitchen table.

"Ma, George was down the block on his own."

"Ma," I shouted, reaching my mother before Joseph could, and I told the whole story about the woman's bag being robbed.

They both looked at us with their mouths open. Da looked over at ma. It was one of those looks that big people have when they don't want to tell yah things.

"Ok George, go out and play and you're not to go down the block on your own, stay with Joseph," da said.

That night I crept up to the sittingroom door and listened. I could hear ma and da talking and moving around. Their voices were muffled by the television. I couldn't make out what they were saying. They're speaking, I'm listening, and I hear them.

"I'm telling yah Maria, what's this place going to be like in a few years? The bottom line is, it's time to go. I'll go into the corporation in the morning and see if they can move us."

The weeks passed quickly, but the cold weather still persisted. Ma pulled a chair away from the kitchen table and sat down. The cold water tap on the tiny sink was dripping. It sounded like a grandfather clock, the one that hung on the wall in my nanny's house in Ballyfermot.

She rose off the chair, walked over to the counter top and watched the kettle boil without saying a word. Then from the counter she picked up a brown envelope. The wooden clothes horse in the sittingroom was full of vests and stockings, so I reached out and took a pair when ma walked in and saw me.

"Leave them George, they're still wet."

Her voice was sombre and there was a quietness about her that was strange. She went to the chest of drawers for clean vests and stockings. Checking our ears before allowing us to get dressed.

"Get washed boys before yah get dressed, not the other way around. People can be poor, but a bar of soap costs yah nothing."

The singing on the radio started up again. I sang along with it and watched ma drink a cup of tea. She opened the envelope again and then turned her attention to me.

"I've wonderful news," she said as she glanced in the long mirror that hung on the wall in the sittingroom.

"Quick George run over to Mrs Crosby and tell her I want her, there's a good boy. Joseph, clear the kitchen please."

There was something up; she never left an untidy kitchen. Her golden rule was never leave a milk bottle on the table, but put the milk in a jug. Ma said it was a sign of poverty.

When Mrs Crosby arrived she was wearing a long cream coat and a scarf on her head.

"What's up Marie, sending for me at this time?"

"There's something I have to tell yah," she said squeezing the letter.

Mrs Crosby looked puzzled.

"We're moving, I just got a letter from the corporation, isn't that great."

"Ah Marie that's wonderful news, it really is. Does Georgie know?"

The word 'moving' suddenly sent alarm bells ringing in my head.

"No, he's gone to work, the letter came after he left. And would yah believe it he was only saying it last night that he might go into the corpo today. Well that's if he gets a chance."

When Mrs Crosby had gone, ma called us into the sittingroom. She sat on the edge of the chair, at first unable to speak with excitement.

"I've great news. We're moving to a new house."

We were not impressed. We didn't want to leave the flat.

"Our friends are here," we protested.

"Well you can come and visit them, and just think about it, you will have a front and back garden, no more climbing stairwells or waiting on lifts that never work."

When da came home from work, he sat down, took off his

jacket, and pulled off his jumper. His armpits were dark after a long day's work.

"Is that heat on, Marie?" he asked while fanning his face with the evening newspaper. Ma was standing at the cooker with her back to him. She turned quickly and da caught her glare.

"Is there something wrong?" he asked worriedly.

It was a bitter cold night outside and I could see the frost gathering on the window. Ma got him his tea in silence, then hastily pulled out the other chair and sat beside him.

"Is there something wrong?" Da asked again, placing his elbow on the table.

"Yeah! Look, we're moving," she replied excitedly, handing him the letter. With these words he pushed his tea away and jumped to his feet. He took her in his arms and they engaged in a warm embrace before dancing around the little kitchen.

"George, open the door a little, the heat in here would kill yah."

"But Da, I'm watching Pippy Long Stockings, and the Clangers is on in a minute."

I walked out and hung my head over the balcony, glancing at the flats and all the washing that lined each one. I listened to the sounds of the streets and boys shouting to their mothers who hung over the balconies calling back to them. The cold made me shiver.

"Come in out of the cold," ma said. It's not good for yah to be going from this heat out to that cold."

"Ok Ma, I'll be in now." I took in a lung full of air and stared up at the moon. It was ever so white, with a real peaceful face.

"Goodbye Mr Moon. Goodbye."

ROUND 4

I opened my eyes, pulled back the sheets, and ran towards the window at the foot of the bed. I could see the pathway that we took to school and the giant tower block in front of us and all the flats behind the skyline. And beyond them was the high grassy wastelands that had hard brown trails of earth cut across them. It was a cold morning.

The bedroom door opened, it was ma.

"Right boys, it's time to get up. We have to leave soon and its time to say goodbye to Peter, John, and little Billy."

Joseph and I were nine years of age, Pat was five, so for us it was sad to say goodbye because the flat was the only home we'd known.

When Joseph and I had washed and finished our breakfast, we walked into our bedroom one last time. Joseph said we were moving because da got a new job. I agreed. Then he said that it was because I'd seen a bag being robbed.

"Marie, Marie," da called.

We rushed to the window when we heard da's voice.

"Make sure yah have everything. I'm watching the furniture down here, Tony will be here soon."

"Ok."

While da was down the block, ma came into the room carrying Pat. She was singing and tiddling him. Secretly I felt a bit excited, wondering what our new home would be like, but Joseph's unhappiness kept me quiet. Ma closed the door and pushed the key through the letter box and we all headed down the block to say goodbye to Mrs Crosby.

When Tony, our father's workmate, pulled up in a big blue Ford van on that cold winter's morning, Joseph and I raced down the steps.

"Well boys, this is a great day," he said, laughing, rubbing his hands over our heads. Tony had a voice, which possessed all the qualities of an upper class man, although his van had a lot of catching up to do.

The wind blew fiercely across the neighbourhood whirling small pieces of paper along the street. They clung to our feet like pieces of elastic bands that wouldn't let go. We finally shook them off and ran to the corner looking over our shoulder at da and Tony loading the van with our belongings.

"Let's play hide and seek," I suggested, tipping Joe's shoulder and running as fast as I could to the corporation bins. I slid in behind them and held my nose. I could see Joe squatting on his hunkers and just by moving slightly, I could see Pat. He was standing on the street in a grey woolly jumper. His dark brown curly hair looked like an afro. There was a mirror of ice lodged on the surface beneath me. I placed my hands on the cold concrete and scaled the wall. I reached the door and I slid in.

There was a noise coming from the basement that sounded like the friction of leather shoes rubbing on the hard tiles. I heard heavy breathing that appeared to be coming from boys who were fighting. I listened with interest as I crept my way into the dark hallway. When I looked in, I saw two boys fighting and I heard a wailing sound. It was coming from a small fat woman. She looked like a washer woman dressed in an apron.

The boys were gaunt in appearance, dressed in dirty clothes and had only bristles for hair. A middle-aged man, who was as long as a tree, stood between them. He had a long coat and a cap. He looked very drunk.

One of the boys slapped the man and when he failed to get any response he kicked the woman. The man fell to his knees. I thought he was going to say a prayer, but he cried instead. The heavyset woman also cried bitterly. The man then rose to his feet, rushed towards one of the boys and lifted him into the air so that his feet couldn't touch the ground. Then he walked him straight into the wall.

My name came to me in a whisper. I turned sharply and saw Joseph.

"Come on, ma and da is looking for yah, we have to go."

So we backed off, out of the darkness and into the light.

My brothers turned the corner. I climbed the stairs to the second floor. Billy was sitting on the ground playing with his old radio. He looked up.

"George."

"Hush Billy, I'm not supposed be here."

He jumped up. We stood face to face.

"I am going to my new house today. You'll get a new house too, Billy."

"Will I?"

"Yeah, we all will."

He flung his arms around me.

"The teacher was mean to yah George. I was sad."

"Yah are me good friend, Billy."

I ran to the door and waved. He waved back and I descended the stairs one last time.

When the van was finally packed, Joseph and I sat in the back, while Pat sat on ma's knee. Crowds of kids gathered around us, filling the streets and the balconies, while all the women were waving from the windows wishing us well.

I noticed Billy among them. A tear ran down my face and when I looked again I thought I saw him wipe a tear from his cheek. I pressed my face against the window and waved. I'm sure I saw him mouth the words,

"Goodbye George."

"Goodbye Billy, sorry for calling yah fat," I said to the glass in front of me.

"Right George, it's time to go," Tony said to our father. "Where is it again Georgie?"

"Finglas South, Tony, I'll show yah." He let down the hand-brake, looked in the mirror and said, "Right, Finglas South, here we come."

ROUND 5

On the northside of Dublin there is a river called 'Clear Water'. To the north of its banks there is a sprawling housing estate of two and three-bedroom houses that is home to a hard-working people. In the early seventies, it was a place of high unemployment. It was a place of narrow streets, high-roofed houses, lanes and alleys, but it was also a place that I called home. The name of this neighbourhood is Finglas South. This is where I would spend the next thirty years of my life.

Sleet had fallen and the rooftops were white. The streets below my bedroom were filled with men, women, and happy children making their way along the slippery roads towards their new homes. Lines of cars and vans arrived and parked on the pavement. The men dropped the bags, rolled up their sleeves and emptied the vans of their belongings.

Joe called. I heard him, but I kept my eye on the streets. There was a man sitting on a cart dressed in a short jacket and cap. He was gazing busily at nothing and didn't see the three boys walking through the crowd, tossing the hats off the smaller kids.

The ringleader stopped, reached out and lay hold of one of his companion's shoulders. The boys looked at one another and fell into a crawling position until they reached the cart. Three pairs of hands reached up and pulled a bag to the ground. The old man turned his head, let out a loud cry and jumped off the cart. But the boys laughed as they reached a corner before vanishing.

Joe called again, I grabbed my coat and hat and rushed down the stairs following him out the door with Pat trailing behind.

"Ma gave us fifty pence," Joe sniggered.

"Great, let's go to the little van down here."

Back then we didn't have shops in South Finglas; we had vans that acted as shops. That's where we were headed.

The streets were alive with people, mostly those who had lived in the tenements of the inner city, the ghettos of Benburb Street, and the flats of Ballymun.

I peeked across the streets and noticed a gang of boys leaning against a wall. They smoked cigarettes, spat on the ground and turned towards us, but we kept walking.

Joe sat crouched on a big rock chewing on his toffee bar. I stood gazing into the streets sucking on a lolly wondering if I would ever see Billy, John, or Peter again. I wondered how far Ballymun was from here.

"Can yah count to ten yet?" Joe asked Pat, as he bit down on the last piece of toffee.

"You just wanna know," Pat replied in long drawn words.

"Well I knew how to count to ten, when I was five-years-old," he replied, sticking out his tongue.

While my brothers were sticking out their tongues to one another, a boy was walking by. Then he turned and passed again, stopping every now and again, looking over at us. I raised my eyes and returned the look.

He was a lean boy with a freckled face and brown hair, dressed in a monkey hat and dark corduroy trousers.

"Hello," he said as he walked across to our side of the street.

"Hello," I replied.

"Will you be my friend? 'Cause I live up there" he said, pointing towards the corner house.

"Yeah," Pat replied, "cause we live down there, and we have Dollypops and Feets."

"My name is Thomas," he said, reaching out his hand.

"I'm George. This is my twin brother Joseph, and the other fella is my brother Pat. From now on you'll be known as Toma."

The freckle-faced kid laughed. "Yeah, and you'll be known as Twinny."

Another freckled-faced kid jumped off a passing cart. He had wild, sticky-up hair, a baggy coat, and trousers that were too short because we could see his stockings.

He looked brazenly into our faces, tipped my shoulder, grabbed Toma's hat and ran like blazes.

"He has your hat."

"Let's go after him," Joseph shouted, and off we went running through the lanes and backyards.

The noise of the streets was barely audible as we scurried up the lane. The icy wind carried a chilling sound as it piled sleet into every corner. We took a deep breath and slid under a fence. The boy was running as fast as he could. He stopped, rested his hand on a wall, inhaled deeply and burst through a back door. The four of us raced after him.

He jumped one wall then another and found himself in another lane. He moved slowly backwards as we moved in. He crouched, then jumped up and tried to run but we grabbed him, pinning him to the wall.

When I looked at him, I noticed he had an unusual way of standing. He held his head back so that his chin was sticking up in the air. And he stared down at us. When I looked at the boys I noticed that they all had their heads held back and chins sticking up, even little Pat was doing it! The silence was broken when Pat said: "How long do we have to stand like this? I am getting a pain."

A winter sun broke through the clouds and cast a goat-like shadow on the wall.

"Here. I have it, Goatee that's it, Goatee," I said. "Your name will be Goatee."

His lips separated and a smile appeared on the strange boy's face.

"Yeah, and what's your names?" he asked, still holding his head in the air.

"I'm Twinny, me brother is the other Twinny, and that's Toma," I said. Pat was dressed in a war suit that he had got for Christmas.

"Yeah and from now on, we'll call him Natzi," Goatee said, pointing to Pat. We shook hands and skipped out of the lane onto the streets, the Twinnies, Toma, Goatee, and Natzi.

A woman called us over and handed us a few apples. Pat skipped ahead of us while the four of us walked with our shoulders held back, heads in the air, passing cars, vans, men, and women, and the gang of boys on the corner.

We played together 'till ma called us in for our tea and then we took turns running up and down the stairs. It was our first night in our new house with our very own stairs that nobody else could walk on but us.

ROUND 6

Toma turned away from his sittingroom window and ran to the door. Toma's house was like ours. The kitchens were large and finished in familiar floor tiles. It was the room where most families lived. The hall was long and narrow and the sittingrooms were so small that people would say:

"Yah wouldn't swing a cat in here."

But I wondered why anyone would want to swing a cat in the first place.

"Are yah coming out to play, Toma?" I asked, skipping up the path with my hands in my pockets.

"Na," he replied, "leave it, me dinner's nearly made and me ma will kill me if I miss it."

"Come on, Joe, Weller, Paulo and Pat are down by the river," I said while tugging at his jumper.

"Right then, wait 'till I get me shoes."

On our way through the neighbourhood, the wind began to pick up. I was glad because it gave us more reason to light a fire.

"Don't tell anyone this," Toma said. "I have a secret."

"What is it?" I asked, as we walked together past the rows of houses and the girls playing relieveo.

"I was playing spin the bottle and guess what? I got a kiss off Sharon O' Neill," he said, with a big grin on his face.

"What was it like? Toma, what was it like?"

"Lollypops, she tasted like lollypops, yah know the green ones yah get in the van for two pence."

Now I was amazed, and wondered if different girls tasted like different lollypops.

"Swear yah won't say a word to anyone because if me ma finds out I'll be kept in 'till I'm twenty."

"I won't say a word, promise."

We followed the road to the fields, eventually making it down to the river. Joe and Weller emerged from behind the large trees. Pat and Paulo stood by the river with the fire lighting. They came from the inner city but moved here the same time as us. Toma was like us, he came from Ballymun.

The sun was a light haze in the distance. The air was so smoky that everything was cast in candyfloss light with a blanket of mist resting just above the river. The smoke was rising onto the street. Joe and Toma ran like Billyo, grabbing some dirt to put it out.

"Yis are mad, the police will be here if they see that," Paulo shouted.

"Here Joe, it's a good time to get chestnuts," Weller said, forgetting that the whole neighbourhood had nearly gone up in smoke behind him.

"Na. I have to get home for me dinner," Toma replied, moving his head from side to side in small jerks.

"Don't worry about that Toma. I know where there's a plot with loads of fresh vegetables," I replied.

"That's a lie," Joe replied.

"Toma kisses girls," I blurted. "Lollypops, he said they taste like lollypops."

"Well I like lollypops," Paulo remarked.

"Is it the red ones yah like?" Weller asked.

Toma looked at me sternly.

"Do you kiss the dollypop woman, Toma?" Pat laughed.

"Na, they kiss me," he replied.

There was a faint moan in Toma's voice as we headed up river towards what we thought were chestnut trees.

Weller picked the cigarettes from his pocket and lit one. He was only ten years old but already smoking. It meant nothing to us that Weller smoked, that's what he did.

We walked for what seemed like a lifetime, across the high grass, and headed down towards the old dusty road that separated one field from another. Toma was wearing a large knitted jumper, the one his ma made. Weller said that the men of Aran wore them when they went fishing; he said he had seen a story all about them on the telly. Toma said that he never saw any men from Aran in his house buying jumpers off his ma.

"Forget about the men of Aran and just keep going," I said.

"I want to go home," Pat cried. "I don't want to see any men from that place. If they don't go to Toma's house they might come to ours."

"Don't worry Pat, ma doesn't make Arans. She only makes cakes and the men from Aran wouldn't eat them anyway."

"My da loves me ma's cakes," Toma said proudly. "Everytime he sees them, he always has the same big smile on his face. And last week when I was playing with me chestnuts, me da pointed to the cakes and whispered."

"Who needs chestnuts when yah can have those rock buns."

The clouds gathered and the wind beat against us as we climbed another hill and headed for the bushes. There was wild grass on both sides of the trees, they were so large that they seemed to reach heaven itself. We crept up and parted the thick weeds that ran between them.

"Creep in behind the trees," Toma shouted, his sense of adventure extending to the point that he really thought we were stars in a cowboy film. Just to be on the safe side, we did what he asked.

The ground was dry, with layers of crisp brown leaves. The autumn air was fresh, filling our nostrils. There were rocks cut like diamonds and the earth opened up like a cave. We sat back and talked about the Alamo and Sitting Bull. Toma said he wanted to be a cowboy like John Wayne. I said I'd like to be an Indian. Weller said that before the world began a man appeared to the Indians. His da told him all about it.

"What was he like?" Joe asked.

"I can't tell. Yis'll be scared."

"Go on tells us," we shouted together.

He told us to move closer and he began to tell us in an urgent whisper.

"His head and hair was as white as snow and his eyes were like a flame of fire."

Weller's voice began to get louder. Pat grabbed my hand. Joe pinched my arm. Toma moved back and Paulo muttered, "I'm not scared."

And Weller continued: "His feet were like bronze, glowing in a furnace and his voice the sound of many waters."

Suddenly we heard a clapping sound. It was drawing near.

"It sounds like a horse coming from the sky," Toma shouted.

"He's coming. He's coming, I want to go home," Pat screamed

Toma jumped over the wild growth, his hands in stand-by position. Weller crawled up behind him like a raccoon. I peered out from behind the bushes and gave a hurried look to the boys. The horse came to a sudden halt and two youths jumped off.

The sound of the pebbles spreading beneath their feet sent chills up our bodies, as we stared blankly at each other. Joe pulled the branch back slightly while the six of us, knotted together by the chins, looked out. The two youths were as big as men.

One of them carried a bottle of cider in one hand and a large stick in the other. They wore tweed coats and low cut shirts. The shirts were partially unbuttoned, displaying large tattoos on their chests. Their jeans were about four inches above their Doc Martins and they both wore long sticky-up hair.

"Wo, wo," said one of the youths grabbing the reins and growling at the beast. The other one beat it with a large stick, hitting his skull so often I imagined his head would fall off. He drank down the last sup of cider and fired it over his shoulder. He walked over to his friend, making a quick motion with his hand, as if he was going to slap him. It was all done in a playful mood. But I didn't want to wait around to see if the mood changed.

Toma stood up, blew the top of his finger as if it was a pistol, and then slid it back into his pocket as if it was a holster.

"Let's hope Toma's guns work," I heard myself say, before jumping over to Pat, as he stood up wheezing for air. I nodded for Joe to move.

Paulo dived on the ground and lay as low as a snake's belly trying to work his way out of the bushes. He cast his eyes back while uncovering a large rock. We followed him through the hole he had made. Once we came out at the other side, we dashed down the steep hill towards the river.

When we reached the riverbed, we breathed a sigh of relief.

"I wasn't scared," Weller stuttered, raising his dark eyebrows, as his hand reached into his pocket for another cigarette. We sat there looking out at the river, thanking our lucky stars. Toma said he felt like John Wayne in *The Sons of Katie Elder*.

"Yeah, I must have missed the part, where John Wayne ran like a rabbit," Joe replied wittily.

"Let's go to Murray's house," I shouted.

"That house is haunted," Toma said, eyes wide as he bit down on his bottom lip.

"There are ghosts up there," Pat screamed.

"Old man Murray hangs people," Weller muttered in a low, barely audible voice.

"I heard that his wife is still hanging in the sittingroom," Joe added.

After a lengthy deliberation, we decided that we would just go close to the house to see if there was really a woman hanging. Toma was a bit reluctant but followed us anyway. So off we trailed up along the dusty road, singing rebel songs, protected by the shelter of the trees. We made our way through the cluster of wild bushes, and a maze of broken cars, until we reached the infamous Scribblestown lane. We kept going without stopping 'till finally we made it to the house.

The old plaster was broken on the outside and there was a little brown fence running around it. We snuck up towards the once-green front door. There were two big oak trees standing on either side. A long rope hung down from one of them. My hair was standing up on the back of my neck. Prickly feelings ran across my body.

We peered through the stained glass panel. In the corner was an old telephone, a large timber staircase, with old carpet down the centre. Underneath was a small door.

"There, I told you he hangs people," Toma screamed, pointing to a length of rope draped across the stairs.

"Here look. That must be the place where he chops people up," I shouted to Joe.

"Be quiet, he'll hear you."

Weller was back in his raccoon position and Toma's guns, once again made an appearance.

"Its time to go, now," Joe screamed. "If the old man doesn't hang us, ma will, if she finds out that we were here."

Suddenly a car pulled up. The wind became more boisterous. Leaves began swirling at our feet. Stories of ghosts, hangings, dark hallways, haunted houses, became too much. We glanced out from the shelter of the house and then looked at each other, after we saw a man jump out of the car. He was running with a shotgun in his hand. In one quick motion he cocked it into the air, pulled back the trigger, and bolted towards us.

His dog ran beside him. We darted around the house. Toma ran in front, Pat fell behind. I grabbed one of his shoulders, Joe grabbed the other and we raced away so fast that his feet didn't touch the ground.

In the distance was a barb wired fence with a hole in the middle. That was our only escape route. Toma went through first. The boys followed. Joe stood on one side. I pushed Pat through to the other side. I gave a hurried glance across the open fields, a cry for help hung on my lips. The dog tore at my heels. But Joe swiftly brought up his boot and the dog backed off and the boys pulled me through.

"Don't even mention John Wayne," I shouted breathlessly at Toma.

"There's not much gain in mentioning John Wayne," he said, tugging at my arm as we made our way towards home, our voices in full flight as we sang two chorus of *The Fields of Athenry*.

When we reached our streets we were greeted with lighthearted chatter, barking dogs and the echo of a mother's voice, calling to her children. As we walked in the hall we could see ma. She was standing at the cooker making dinner.

She looked over at us while pouring the water off the spuds. Her eyes could tell us things before her words reached our ears.

"Don't sit down at that table with those hands, go upstairs, and wash them," she said, as she placed the pot on the edge of the sink. We rushed out the door and up the stairs making more noise than a galloping stampede of wild horses.

Later in the evenings, when darkness fell, ma would sit us down on the little rug in front of the open fire. It was here we got a front-row view of the lives that our grandparents had lived. She began by telling us a story about our grandmother who came from a little village in Donegal, from well to do stock.

In 1912, at the age of thirteen she was ready to set sail on the Titanic. Her bags were loaded on the horse and cart, ready to take the long trip across to Belfast to board the infamous ship. But she was informed at the last minute that she couldn't go, so she ran out of the house.

The summer breeze ran beside her as she passed the lush landscape carved into overhanging oak trees and long grass. When she reached a fallen tree that had found its home among the blackberries, she rested. It was there that she settled her mind and rested her hopes for a future in Ireland. She never did climb the stairs of the infamous Titanic and our fate was sealed.

In 1922 at the age of twenty-three, she left her home and went to live in Dublin. There she met a man by the name of Thomas Stafford. He was just coming to terms with the death of one of his brothers, who died during the 1916 Rising. They later married and lived in the tenements of Gardiner Street.

Alfie Byrne, the Lord Mayor of Dublin, moved a lot of people out to Ballyfermot at that time. My mother, who was born there in Ballyfermot, was the youngest of five children.

In the year 1834, just before the Famine years in County Kildare, John Fitzgerald was born, my great-great-grandfather. He lived through the Famine years and witnessed the plight of the Irish. He watched as the masses made their way towards the coffin ships at Queenstown.

By 1864 his son Patrick was born, and the only son born to him was our grandfather, Patrick jnr. In 1931 he entered training for the priesthood, but later abandoned his vocation and joined the army. He met Helen Keating, a beautiful dark haired girl who came from Dublin's Liberties. The eldest son born to them was George, my father.

"Right boys it's time for bed," da said as ma finished one of her stories.

We kissed da and ma and climbed the stairs to bed. A few minutes later I heard the door open and big people talking, the door closed, and I heard ma and da talking

My bedroom door opened and both of our parents walked in, calling Joseph and me at the same time. Da gave out a little cough, the ones big people give when they haven't got a cough!

"Ok boys, yah know little Billy who lives in Ballymun."

Our eyes lit up and we stared at one another shouting, "Can he come over to stay? Can he, Ma ? Can he? Please Da."

"No son, he can't," he said, after he gave another little cough, "because he's gone to heaven."

The room suddenly went silent. Joe looked at me, our lips quivering.

"Is he gone to heaven?" Joe asked.

In my minds eye, I could see him jumping up and down saying, "that's the tu-tu Santa's bringing me." I saw him waving on that cold winter's day from the balcony of Ballymun.

Ma walked over and hugged us while da stood behind us rubbing our backs as we both cried bitterly. Little Billy was killed after he fell off the back of a lorry he shouldn't have been on. He never got to drive the big tu-tu's he said he would drive when he got to be a big boy.

"Is he a hero now? He said someday he was going to be a hero, his granda even told him."

"Yeah, he is a hero," ma said sadly. When ma and da left I wondered if he would remember me when I got to go to heaven. "Dear God, tell Billy that one day when I get to tell stories, I will tell all the people about him," I sobbed wondering if John and Peter would be ok. And then I fell asleep.

ROUND 7

By the summer of 1975, we had grown accustomed to our neighbourhood. In my childhood memory, there are growing boys running, laughing, swimming in rivers, picking apples off trees on hot carefree summer days. These days ended with campfire stories, about the heroes of the neighbourhood.

It was on one of those hot summer days when the Missy One called me. She was sitting on the front step of her house with the hall door wide open. Now if the Missy One called yah, well yah didn't say no.

She was the size of a baby whale, had four chins and hands like shovels. People said that she could kill a man, and it was said that she once killed a dog. Toma said that the dog story wasn't true, it was a cat and anyway the cat was half dead. Weller said it didn't matter if the cat was half dead because cats have nine lives. I said, who cares, if she killed a cat or a dog, the point is, could she kill us? Toma and Weller agreed on this point.

"Georgie will yah go the van for us? Here get's a loaf of bread, a bag of potatoes, and two loose smokes. Ask him for Woodbines and there's twenty-five pence over, yah can keep it. Thanks love. Make sure it's a loaf, that's all me da eats."

I had the money in my hand and both hands in my pockets as I skipped along down the street.

"How yah George?" Margo shouted from across the road. I felt a funny tingly feeling because I liked Margo. She had black raven hair, beautiful eyes like Cleopatra, and a friendly smile.

"I am going to the van for the Missy One, she gave me twenty five pence, and I'll buy yah a lollypop," I said. Then I had a secret thought: *maybe I'll get a kiss and find out what lollypop she tastes like. I hope it's red because that's my favourite colour.*

"Thanks George," Margo replied, as I skipped past her, and ran across the sprawling housing estate towards the van. It was evening time, and still the sun was being kind to us.

In the middle of one of the blocks of houses was a lane. It led into the neighbouring road. A small group of boys raced around, pulling at each other, dogs ran wild and barked at passing cars. The sky was clear, and the smell of fish being cooked in a neighbour's house filled the air.

A man was dancing in the street to the sound of music that floated out of an open window. The kids made a circle around him and cheered him on, but I kept my distance because I was a bit scared of him. He was always drunk and he made very scary faces that I thought might give me nightmares again! I didn't want to look at him for too long, so off I skipped down the street trying to think of something nice.

"Toffo that's it, Toffo, think of Toffo," I muttered.

"What did she ask me to get her again?" I asked myself.

I racked my brains and then it came to me. "Potatoes, yeah, that's what she asked for."

Back then most families had the same diet. Potatoes on Monday to Friday, with an added bonus of receiving them on Saturday and ending off with a special treat of them on a Sunday. But right then it wasn't potatoes that were on my mind. Something else had caught my attention - Snookerball!

His eyes were like balls of fire that could set you ablaze with just one look. His head was scalped and there was a pink scar that ran from the back of his neck to his forehead, hence the name Snookerball.

He was a child of the streets who dismissed all authority. He never liked or trusted anybody. I remembered the winters morning I saw this boy smash the bottom windows of his mother's house. I watched him from the shadows. His mother chased after him with a rolling-pin in her hand. She was thin and all impoverished looking, even as a kid I could see that.

Snookerball had already seen the inside of a reform school, a career that would take him to the big house, a career that would eventually lead him to the capital crime of murder. But for now, he wasn't the State's problem, he was mine.

The lapping sound of the streets still pervaded the air, with the laughing children and the music, that came from the open windows. But I was drawn away, called as it were to focus, on the 'shoeshine boy' who carried a blade.

Snookerball locked his eyes on me as he stood with his back laid against the wall. He then sat on his hunkers without speaking. I stole a look as I tried to pass and when I did, I noticed that he was standing on his feet again.

"Here gis you're odds," he bawled clenching his teeth so violently that his face twisted.

I groped the wall and began to walk backwards. He growled. I went to run, he ran after me. He grabbed my collar, dragged me back, and struck me across the jaw. Dogs barked, doors shut softly, and I fell onto the rocks with the scent of blood in my nostrils.

A small mousy-faced kid with light brown hair stood beside him. He was all fearful, laughing at his jokes whether he thought they were funny or not. He looked at me for a moment and then ran.

It would give me no greater pleasure to tell you that I jumped up and fought back bravely, like the characters that existed in my imaginary world, warriors that fought off great monsters, and overcame them, gallant men running across forest to win the fair lady. But in truth, lying on the ground amidst the rubble and the blocks was a child who was afraid of ghost stories, the boogie man, and even the man that appeared on the Sandeman bottle!

He picked me up and shook me violently until I dropped the money. Our tight embrace was shattered, as stones were hurled towards us. It was Sausage, a kid my own age who lived down the block. Suddenly an army of children rushed past shouting,"Davy's been hit with an axe. Davy's been hit with an axe. Quick, hurry."

A crowd gathered as I slowly walked out of the lane. There were many faces around me. Faces of kids I knew, faces of strangers. But as I stared through the crowd I shivered when I saw the ghastly figure of Snookerball glance back at me. The crowd ran towards the school to see if Davy was ok. I watched Sausage run ahead of Snookerball and slip into another lane.

Davy survived the attack and many more. But little Sausage's broken body would be found face down in a lane, beaten to death, at the age of twenty-nine. Left there by a gang he couldn't run away from.

Micko will grow up. And when he does he will kill two people. Snookerball will also become a murderer and spend the best part of his life behind bars. But the boy will become a man, and his naked body will swing lifeless against a wall.

See Kojak didn't walk these streets. But the gangs of New York did. They just had a different name.

ROUND 8

It was a long hot summer; well that's how I remember it. The neighbourhood was enveloped in the sounds and language of our streets which rushed through the open window of my bedroom.

I placed my hands on the white sills and caught a butterfly. It's soft velvet like wings brushed off my palms. I opened them and blew gently, releasing the little creature. It spread its wings and for a moment it hung out there, in mid-air.

The colours were radiant, freckled yellow sown into a blood red. It hovered gracefully with the pale blue sky as its backdrop. And then it said goodbye, flying away in glorious freedom.

The sun was still high firing short shadows into the room. I noticed Mattie standing at the corner with a sports bag placed at his feet. He waved up to me so I waved back.

"I'm going boxing, are yah into going?" he shouted.

"Na," I shouted back before closing the window.

I climbed onto the bed and looked at the ceiling and began to count the nail holes. This wasn't the first time I had the pleasure of meeting people like Snookerball. I met them on a daily basis in the schoolyard and on the streets.

The sound of a fly buzzing around the room disturbed me. Its legs tipped my nose as it tried to use it as a resting place. I began to flap my hands into the air and as I jumped out, chasing it around the room, squeaking sounds came from the floorboards.

I shook my head, grinned and I walked back to the bed.

"Boxing, I can't even kill a fly," I heard myself say.

Then I had an idea. I sat on the bed waiting for the fly to appear again. My thinking was that if I could catch the fly, maybe I could become a boxer.

I positioned myself holding my arm outstretched and fingers spread. The light spun. The fly appeared. I sprung into the air and caught the intruder in one grasp, and it fell to the ground.

Rushing down the stairs as if I'd received a sign from God I burst into the sittingroom.

"Ma, Ma, can I join the boxing club with Mattie, please, Ma." Da was sitting on the chair with the newspaper. He turned full circle to where ma was standing. The silence that says more than words entered the conversation and the answer came, it was no. After much persuading and begging I sensed they were giving in.

"Who's going?" "What time is it starting at?" "What time will yah be home?" they both asked. Eventually I was given a six months trial basis, so now I was taking the first steps to becoming a boxer.

♪

On the night I was joining the Glasnevin Boxing club back in 1975, Mattie was waiting on the corner while my parents stood in the front garden waving us off. I imagined their eyes would follow us all night and I was horrified when Mattie told me that the older boys had gone ahead. I was never to allow this information fall from my lips especially in the presence of me ma and da, and I told Mattie in no uncertain terms that he should never speak it either. He agreed and off we went.

We jumped off the bus at Harts Corner, walked past Smurfits and turned onto Prospect Avenue, heading down the winding streets and lanes that came out at Decorsie Square.

Mattie moved along at rapid speed while I followed close on his heels, passing the main street until we finally made it on to Mobhi Road down a narrow lane, and there it was - the boxing club.

The club occupied a small space that was situated beside a river, only a few feet away from the picturesque Botanic Gardens. It had been built some thirty or so years before. A line of small windows ran along the one side, the roof was flat, and the front door walked out onto a lane.

When I stepped through its doors, I entered a world within a world, where the unwritten rule was, hit them first, and hit them hardest. It was a rule that was engraved on the hearts of these men. Men who had broken noses and wore scar tissue as trophies!

The walls and ceiling were dull; age had coated them in atmosphere, and there was a musty smell so thick, it was tangible. Across the floor, at the far wall there was an old wooden table upon which was set lines of well-worn boxing gloves, oxblood with the occasional black pair set among them. I stared, it was unbroken, and then I fixed my gaze on a boy who walked out of the dressing rooms. He was lean but strong-looking with a solitary look. His body was a tool, a weapon that moved at ease, punching the bag at the speed of light.

A voice calling time-out caught my attention. Switching my glance, I caught sight of an old man standing outside the ring. He was resting his arm on the top rope, his hair was cropped, and he had a strong narrow build for a man of his age. He turned quickly and caught sight of me. I lifted my hand and waved. He turned towards the ring, and I stood there feeling like an idiot.

He then made a gesture with his hand for me to go over to him. When I did, I noticed two of his fingers were missing. He grinned, shook my hand and told me to call him Danny.

Suddenly I was surrounded by a group of young boys of my own age. They wore tracksuits too big, T-shirts too small, and there wasn't a blade of hair between them. It all took me by surprise. I was overwhelmed by their kindness.

They shook my hand for so long that I thought I might not leave there until I was twenty. But the guy with the narrow shoulders bid them to return to their station which they did obediently.

One of the boys carried my bag into the dressing room. He was very helpful emptying the bag of all its contents. But when he saw that there was nothing of value, he adopted a different attitude and left hastily. I imagined that something else might have been on his mind when he never said goodbye, or maybe he knew he would see me later.

Changing quickly, I walked out of the dressing room. The old cracked timber floor was drenched with pools of sweat and stained with blood of young boys and men. Hairless men joined in their quest for victory in a world where only the strong survive.

After I had a few words with the old man, Danny, I was out on the wooden floor, throwing punches into mid-air, not really knowing what I was doing. It didn't matter. I felt part of something. The only thing that separated me from everyone else was that they could fight and I couldn't.

A few weeks had passed since I had joined the club and I felt I was beginning to pick things up. A blustering wind blew into the damp run-down gym, creeping in through the badly hung door. I dragged myself away into the corner towards an old mirror and I began to copy the boys who were shadowboxing.

The smoke from the cigarette circled above Danny's head as he scanned the gym looking for sparring partners. I watched him hand pick a tough- looking kid, with tight black hair and a bulls nose. He was the type of kid who I'd say only smiled on birthdays. And I'd say even then that would be forced!

He was of stocky build and his arms were hanging down by his side with bandages on both hands. He walked towards the ring slowly like a gladiator about to enter the arena.

A growling voice left his body. It was directed towards a little kid that stood in front of him. The boy looked up and squinted as if a wind had blown in his face. Next he ran across the floor, and disappeared behind a punch bag.

Sourface climbed into the ring dressed in laced boots that enclosed strong legs complete with thick calves that looked like they belonged to a body-builder.

"George," Danny called. His words were more chilling than the wind that blew beneath me. He didn't have to repeat himself.

I walked across the gym like a man walking the plank, aware of all the eyes that surrounded me. It was a hard road to walk, but I knew it was a necessary one, especially if I wanted to develop in a sport that makes no apology for broken noses and crushed bodies. I was now ten years old.

Danny grinned and gave a little chuckle as he placed the eight-ounce brown leather gloves on me; I stood up from the small wooden stool that was at the side of the ring.

When I stepped in, I felt a sudden shock. This was no back lane fight. These boys could fight and they were experienced in delivering punches without mercy. The heavy chain that held up the punch bag made a rattling sound as it jerked from left to right, springing into an air that was impregnated with a damp odour.

I saw old newspaper clippings that were hanging on the wall. I wondered how old they were, and I wondered if the boxers that appeared in them were any good. Then I looked at my sparing partner and wondered how I was going to get out of there alive! I think that's what made me more nervous. But this was no time for reading old newspapers as my opponent came at me, shuffling his feet, and jabbing.

The colour left my cheeks and my lips began to work themselves into a usual position my top lip curling up like Elvis!

"Now keep your hands up kid," the kind gentleman said, in a low voice.

"I think I know what to do," I muttered, talking more to myself. "Run like blazes."

My head bolted back as the leather gloves went crashing against the side of my face. Any hopes for quick success were soon dashed when I went scrambling to the canvas. Sourface stood over me with his legs in a V shape. I was in a more S shape - S for Swiss roll - because I was curled up like one!

Danny called time to end the round. I walked back with my head hanging. When I raised it, the boy was glaring at me. Catching hold of the end of his glove he pulled it up with his teeth and placed the thumb on one of his nostrils and blew violently. Danny lifted the rope. I stepped out and met another-gentleman who went by the name of Rocky. He stood there as if he was waiting on me to ask him a question. But I had no questions. I descended the steps into the dressing room and sat on the bench in silence. But the silence vanished quickly because all of a sudden I was surrounded by many faces, faces of all the friends that I had met. They had a quieter attitude about them.

The door opened again and I saw another face. I watched his movements, and the hardness of his features. My mind dressed itself in fresh thinking and it was then I knew that boxing wasn't only about skill, but attitude.

The dressing room emptied itself quickly of all the boys. I was left alone to gaze timidly around. I overheard muttering.

"Danny throw that kid out, he'll never amount to much," an

older boxer said.

I looked at the gloomy walls and switched my glance to all the papers that were scattered across the floor, remembering the master's words.

"Mr Fitzgerald, you'll never amount to much. Boys from the bad rows never do."

The words sunk heavily into my heart. I sighed deeply and crept out.

Danny was alone with a tall sweeping brush in his hand. I stopped and looked directly at him. He sat at the side of the ring and took a drag on his smoke.

"You're disappointed? See kid, in the boxing game there's no winners or losers, just fighters. Boys who are brave enough to climb through those ropes," he said.

I just stood, looking at the floor.

He pulled his face from me and looked into the ring, as if he was searching for himself or even a shadow that would remind him that he was one of those boys. But that time was long gone and all that was left was the old man. And somehow even as a kid I saw his thought. But he was a man of few words and they were the things he would never tell you.

"Can I come back again?" I asked, tugging at the old fighter's jacket.

"Yep, see you on Monday," he replied with a grin. "If yah come back, ye'll make it as a fighter, because that will tell me that ye've got heart," he shouted after me.

"Thanks," I replied, running out into the lane.

At the top of the lane the boys stood waiting on me. But before I could reach them they started slagging me.

"Go home by yer self, yah cry ba, yah loser, here George spell loser."

They laughed and ran off.

I moved with great speed through a maze of streets until finally I ended up at Decorcie Square again. I stood on a corner remaining silent long enough to catch my breath and thought of the boys inside that world, who had no hair, well-worn track-suits, boys who could fight.

I wondered about the things the kind man said and then wondered about the word 'heart'. He said I could get it on Monday, so I was glad that Monday wasn't far off. Then as my mind drifted, I thought about fighting, a thing I wasn't sure I'd be able to do. But as the wind blew against me, one thing was clear. Tonight I'd had my first real encounter with the angels with dirty faces!

ROUND 9

Mr O'Brien, our master, walked up and down in front of the class talking out aloud about God, the holy mother, and especially Christian Brothers, who he said reared him.

He told us that he was grateful to the kind Christian Brothers for beating the tar out of him and told us that if any of us moved an inch, he would beat the tar out of us.

Then he told us that boys are always grateful to God when the tar was beaten out of them. He took a long pause and picked his nose. He would pick his nose and produce a smile, a proud smile that was self-gratifying after bestowing on us this kind information.

"It's a free country, and everyone is entitled to an education, thanks be to the kind Government, that every man is allowed move freely about this country. "Don't even blink, Mr. Fitzgerald when I am talking. I know what goes on in the minds of boys who blink too much."

"Yes Sir, sorry sir, for blinking in this free country."

He stood still with his shoulders shrugged up to his ears and he looked so stiff that he reminded me of a mummy. There was another long pause, during which all the boys were plunged into a state of fear. Then he spoke again and we knew for sure he was still alive.

"It's ok, Mr. Fitzgerald, boys are allowed to blink in this free country as long as they have a good reason to blink. Have you got a good reason for blinking?"

"I have sir."

"Well, that's ok then."

"Right, open up your Irish books before I cut the backsides off yis."

The boy that sat in front of me was not too happy to know that his backside could be cut off him, so he called up to O'Brien.

"Cut the back side off me and me da will be up te box the jaw off yah!"

Our master was a strong army-looking man with thick wavy hair and plump red cheeks, but all of a sudden he went pale. He picked up the duster, threw his arm back, and fired with all his might. Luckily, he missed.

"It's hung yah should be, hung by the neck," he screamed before charging at him like a bull.

I sat frozen in my seat with my mouth open wide trying desperately not to blink. I watched the madman lift Fitzer into the air by the locks and walk him slowly across the classroom. The boy kicked and screamed. The master stopped at the top of the class. The door flung open. The boy's big brother appeared.

"Get da, Whacker get da," Fitzer roared.

A few minutes later a small Italian looking man rushed in. He walked over to the master and gave him a box to the delight of all the boys.

"If he puts his hand on yah again, come around, and get me," he shouted and walked out.

I raised my hand and asked to go to the toilet.

"Get into that corner you sorry excuse for a boy," O'Brien shouted. I stood there crouched over, holding my private parts; I couldn't resist it, so I stole a look at O'Brien, holding his jaw.

Little Pete went to the toilet, but he could do that anytime because he had one of those bag things! My eyes followed him and just as he left, the door opened again. This time a muscular boy was pushed into our class. Behind him was his master. He had used the F-word to his master and to anyone who he saw looking at him. The boy that sat next to me was called Heffo, he had freckles like Toma. He stood up and said, "F-you," to the boy at the wall, "and F-your ma."

Mr O'Brien ran down the class and swung Heffo around like a rag and then he gave Martin a box. Everybody was using the F -word or getting swung around or getting boxes and I was on my knees holding my private parts.

"John," Mr O'Brien shouted, to the boy that was brought into our class. "By the time I'm finished with yah, ye'll have a backside like a tomato."

"F- you and tomatoes," he said, as he ran out the door and out of the school.

Broken faces, backsides cut off, and hung by the neck! I could-n't hold any longer so I ran to the toilet. It was all worth it I thought as I stood in the little cubical.

The smell of smoke still lingered in the hallway as it was only a few weeks since the school was broken into and badly burned; it was on the news and in all the newspapers.

Outside I could hear a priest and nun singing and then I heard my name — "Mr Fitzgerald."

"Yah blaggard, that's what yah are, another thug in from Finglas South. Yis are nothing but trouble. Come with me," he said as he rushed me up along the corridor, past the singing nun and priest.

"Genuflect in front of the holy people," he blasted, pushing me to my knees.

"Yes Sir," I replied as my knees touched the ground.

"Sorry for interrupting your prayer Father, Reverend Mother, but I must be on my way," the master said in a much softer voice.

He lifted me up and rushed towards the principal's office. He knocked twice.

"Come in," said the voice.

Mr O'Brien was a very stern man that everyone feared. Anyone who gave trouble in the school was brought to him. A boy had absconded from the school and that was the real reason I was in the principal's office. The boys from Finglas South were the new kids on the block. The school we attended was in a different part of Finglas.

Mr O'Brien growled. It was a fierce growling that sounded like that of a bear with a sore head. He ranted about John, the other boy from the South who later in life would become my friend.

The principal didn't seem to be paying him too much attention, but glared at me angrily. Then the discussion started about me.

"So does this boy have any aspiration for the future?"

"He does sir; he once remarked under his breath that he would like to write stories."

"When I get older sir," I cut in.

"See what I mean. The boy's head is full of silly nonsense. It's not all together his fault, if you know what I mean. He's a twin and although his twin is bright, maybe his gift is in another area."

"Oh I see... remedial," the principal remarked.

"Borderline," O'Brien replied.

"Right, take the boy back. As for the other scallywag, when you get your hands on him, leather him as hard as you can, and if that doesn't do it we'll see about removing him. "It would be best if all these new boys from that area could be removed, but sure, we'll live with them for now."

"Ok sir, come on Fitzgerald."

The Master opened the door and we walked along the corridor.

"See Mr Fitzgerald, always be thankful to God and his mother for the good teachers you have. And put away that nonsense of writing, it's not for you."

"Yes sir, thank you sir," I replied.

I was sitting at the window when I saw John again. He was jumping over the walls in the gardens across the street, and then he disappeared. I thought about what Mr O'Brien said. Then ma's words whispered in my ear. "If at first yah don't succeed try and try again."

I glanced up at the blackboard and I read a commandment from the Bible. It read, 'Honour thy father and mother'.

The bell rang ending school and we rushed out the door like men who had just been given their freedom. Holding our noses we disappeared into the dark concrete tunnel. A line of work men were standing beside the pipe as we ran through. Just in front of the church, another gang of men had placed a long plank across a large hole that had been dug. So I crossed it, fencing my way to victory, with Robin Hood and Little John at my side. I drove myself without mercy, slaying all the armies imaginable.

Crawling out of the Sheriff's dungeon, I galloped off across the moist earth in the company of the Merry Men.

"Here George, lets take a break," Joe shouted, as we headed to our usual resting place.

"Don't forget Woody Woodpecker is on at three a clock," Toma said.

Nobody answered because we had our eyes on Bob who was walking home resting his school bag on his head. We kept our eyes on him until he disappeared between the houses.

Then we sat on the large granite steps that ran along the side of the church.

Goatee would often meet us there, as we engaged in stories about boxing and the art of fisticuffs. Goatee, the long-legged kid, had four main characteristics. He had an overwhelming ability to engross himself in stories that had no bearing on what we were talking about. Secondly, he had the uncanny ability to convert our conversations from reality to an imaginary world; thirdly, he consistently referred to everyone as 'brother' and finally, his slippery fingers!

He was the type of kid who kept in his drawer photographs he never had, passports he'd never seen, pencilling out the shadowy parts of his life with his giant imagination.

Sitting under the afternoon sun that day our appetites began to grow, due largely to the smell that was coming from the little bakery not far away. Goatee stood up and launched into another powerful story, that had no bearing on boxing or ring craft for that matter.

A tall dark haired girl, who was a couple of years older, passed us. She smiled at me. Goatee couldn't take his eyes off her as he studied her with his mouth open. So I reached over and gently closed it! I don't think he even noticed. Straight away he recited to us about the girl he'd met.

His story entailed large palm trees, sandy beaches and bright blue seas, not forgetting the baby-faced girl with the long black hair, and the pencilled-in eyelashes.

The story bore an incredible resemblance to one of the television soaps from a few days before. In my mind's eye, I could see an Egyptian queen standing in front of a massive ship, cut from the finest timber, pleading her undying love for Goatee.

"She resembled a movie star," he said, "with green eyes and pencilled-in lashes." When Goatee pointed her out, Toma laughed.

"She looks like a movie star alright, the type that haunts houses," Toma said.

After a little investigating by Toma, it turned out that the girl didn't even know who Goatee was. But for now, sitting in the sunlight, Goatee's story thrilled us. With all his shortcomings, he was a loveable fellow. In short, he was our friend. After he had besieged us with yet another story, he suddenly took off without saying a word.

We jumped off the granite stone and began to make our way home, heading across the village towards the bridge. I had a sneaking suspicion that the aroma of the freshly baked cakes which had swam down towards us earlier, had overwhelmed him.

He wasn't the little Catholic boy, who believed in hell and damnation and man's fall from grace. He believed, if you could make yourself invisible, you could help yourself to anything that wasn't nailed down. He also believed you weren't responsible for it, because the fact was, you weren't there!

The four of us climbed the bridge from the outside. A gush of wind that came from a passing truck sent a chill up our backs. When we felt it was too dangerous we jumped over to safety.

We cut through the lanes and reached the grassy fields. There we sat for a moment, resting our backs against the trees.

"Tell us one of your stories George," Weller asked.

"Right, once upon a time there was this 'ogre' that lived in a faraway land. His house was hidden in an old tree. The little men looked up at him and wondered if he was awake or asleep."

Everyone lifted their eyes and looked up at the tree just about the same time a dark cloud hovered over us.

"When he saw the men he chased after them 'till he caught them and when he did he boiled them in his big pot before eating them."

Toma jumped to his feet and lifted a stick into the air as if it was a sword. His hand looked frozen as he pointed it towards the sky.

"Fear not me good men for the king is coming riding upon a white horse. His name is written upon his thigh and a mighty army of heaven is with him."

"Look the return of the king, let's fight," Joe said as we all jumped up fencing each other.

"Stop, stop," Weller shouted.

"What's wrong with yah now?" Toma asked, throwing his stick away.

"We killed them. Look!" He said pointing to an army of dead slugs.

We stopped and looked down on them.

"Woody Woodpecker will be on soon," Toma remarked.

"Yeah, but let's bury these first," Weller said.

Toma threw his eyes up in the air, picked up his stick and we dug a few graves and laid them to rest. Then we rested again. Toma was tugging at my jumper demanding my attention while Weller lit up another cigarette.

"What do you want Toma?" I said. I looked up and caught Joe's glare as he stood above the lane.

"Come'ere. Come'ere."

His word came to us in a whisper and he motioned with his hands for us to be quiet. When we came near to him, we saw what had grabbed his attention. There he was, the long legged-kid, walking up the lane, his face smudged in cream.

In his hands was a cardboard box, filled with fresh cream cakes. Unaware of our presence, he munched the cakes like a man eating his last meal. He saw us and shouted: "Are you dressed for dinner gentlemen?" as he prepared a sit-down meal and toasted us with a large apple pie.

We munched on afternoon dessert in the sunlight as we laughed at Toma's jokes and Goatee's stories. After our meal he reached into his back pocket, pulled out a pack of crushed smokes and tossed one to Weller.

"You're a quick worker," Weller said as he lit up his smoke.

"Na just invisible, that's all brother."

As it turned out, he just jumped the small counter, grabbed the tray, and dashed out the door.

"Would you cry if yah got locked up?" Toma asked sheepishly.

"Haven't yah heard Toma," he replied, his hand resting on his head, while puffing his smoke towards the clear blue sky.

"Hard men don't cry. That's what brother."

Goatee was the first to jump up, his bowels calling for attention. He ran down the steep hill, but he wasn't alert as he should have been because he didn't see the rough-faced kid who was heading in his direction.

A whipping sound skimmed through the air and a thick branch crashed off Goatee's skull. He backpedalled with his hands over his head but no tears came. Another branch then cut through the air and caught him on the back of the head causing it to bleed.

We stood on the top of the hill and watched him being reduced to a puppy. I scooped up a handful of dirt and raced down the dry bank. I fired it, distracting the bully-boy for a moment. Goatee rushed into him like a bull, knocking him to the ground. We were then on our toes as if the hounds of hell were chasing us. Toma reached the streets first. We looked back and saw Goatee limping and bloody, so we went back and helped him get out of there. We walked home at the same pace singing '*Josie was my woman*'. It was Toma's favourite song.

After our tea we played together, until a couple of neighbours invited us to participate in their version of the Olympic Games. When the signal was given we charged through the streets as if we were running for gold. Git Fay, Ray Byrne, and Beanie were the master minds behind the games. Toma almost always won but it was always a tough competition between him and Git. The girls from our road never participated, but they did cheer us on.

A few hours afterwards we were playing with the makeshift trolleys when Jimmy Boy O' Rourke came running up the street shouting, "Goatee's being chased, Goatee's being chased."

Leaving our trolleys, we ran to the corner and saw him jumping over garden walls in his short trousers, being chased by a guard in short sleeves. He fell to the ground and was grabbed up.

Goatee's ma, a stocky woman, was standing at the broken gate, with tears flowing down her face. Mothers called their children in and closed their doors, while all alone, she stood catching a glimpse of the car that held her eldest boy.

These streets were a school teacher to so many. He had crossed the threshold of petty crime to more serious lawbreaking. We stood there and watched as our friend turned towards us, his eyes looked sad his face looked helpless.

Where was Goatee's father? He was working every hour God sent to feed his eight children, in a time of low wages and high taxes.

But for the rest of us the stars would light up the night sky. And we'd wish upon them. Then one by one we would be called in. Dreamy-eyed, the day fully spent, hearts satisfied, we'd separate. There were different numbers on our doors but in many ways we were all one big family.

ROUND 10

My hands were tightly fitted with light brown bandages as I threw punches outside the newly built ring. Danny swung his hands across my head in a clockwise rhythm.

"Left right left," he called, moving closer.

Inside the ring a contest was taking place. One of the young boy's fighting was Goatee. He had got off with a warning from the judge. By this time Joe, Weller and Paulo had also joined the club.

"Right son, you're warm enough now," Danny said in his usual comforting way.

"Do you think I can win, Danny?" I asked, as if he could somehow promise the result.

"It's not about winning kid. It's about boxing," he replied, adding: "All yah need to do is keep on top of him. Don't give him any room to move."

When I looked across the ring I got the first glimpse of my opponent. It was Sourface the kid that left me like a doormat a year back. I hadn't seen him since he left our club and was I glad! I watched him walk behind his coach as they went into the dressing room.

I snuck into my dressing room and listened to the sound of the pads being punched. The sound was alarming. It had that ring to it, telling me that he was really a champion.

I looked in the mirror and checked my teeth, wondering if I would have the same amount when I left the ring. I took out my bandages, pushed my thumb through the hole and wrapped them around my fist. The humming sound of voices was rising outside. I waited. Time was drawing near. Not too long now. My heart began to race. I could feel my palms sweating as I walked across the floor. The bell outside rang. The crowd went silent. The door opened and Danny stuck his head around.

"Right son you're up next."

I took a deep breath and walked out. I could hear the referee counting to ten. My heart jumped and then I saw Goatee lying on his back. Sadly, Goatee lost. I was next and I became extremely frightened by the whole idea.

A year had passed since my first sparring session in which I'd spent every moment I could spare, sculpturing my body into a fighting machine. I trained in a world where every muscle was used, either to your loss or your gain. Defeat was my enemy. I would pound the heavy bag until my hands bled, and skip until my legs felt numb.

"Right son, up you go," Danny said, pointing to the steel steps that led up to the ring.

Shrugging my shoulders from left to right, I threw a flurry of punches. Feelings of apprehension overwhelmed me. Danny stood behind me and gently pulled me towards him.

"Now listen kid, this ring is bigger than you're used to. Don't give him any room, like I said, keep on top of him," he said in a commanding voice.

Seconds out - round one, the bell rang.

I ran out firing left and right hands using speed as my ultimate weapon.

A solid right hand woke me up, sending me back a few steps. But Danny was right, I had heart. I made my way through the first round and walked back to my corner. It was during the second round right in the middle of the ring that something happened and everything came together. I avoided the wild swings that were coming at me by sliding underneath, and when I did, I saw that his hands were low. So I walked in but I didn't go it alone, I brought a left hook and right hook with me.

Bang, wallop, the stars arrived, tiny sparklers appearing before him. I moved around the ring dancing like Bo Jangles. He ran for cover, I cut him off. He couldn't relax. I pressed forward, like a man hunting wild game.

He looked subdued but still threw his best shots. They came at me in a great number, but were fruitless. I moved my head slightly and escaped each time, rushing in with a left and right hand. His head was bowed. The referee stepped in and held me back, stretching his arm across my chest.

Outside the old journeymen were on their toes with their caps, jackets, braces, and polo shirts; images painted in my mind like, the men sitting on the Brooklyn Bridge.

"Box on," the ref shouted.

I threw a right hand, it was a short snappy right hand, but when it landed, my duty was done. My first fight was a win and Joe also won.

"That kid you just beat was a league champion."

"Are you sure Danny?" I said excitedly.

"Yep." That's all he said. The old wise man often used just one word, but it said a lot.

Outside the night was fresh and clear. We ran to the car. An old boxing trainer who wore a cap and braces called me.

"Hey kid, what's your name?"

"George Fitzgerald," I replied, turning towards him.

"I'll remember that," he said as the car sped off down the lane.

Danny turned towards us, as he was sitting in the front passenger seat.

"There are two things you need in this world boys - your fists and your name. Work on them and you will dominate the fight game."

♪

I opened my eyes, pulled back the blankets, and dived into the bathroom with my brothers following behind. After we washed, we chased each other around the bedrooms. The clothes went up in the air and the pillows flew around the room. Then, we walked into the kitchen like lambs.

Patches of the early morning sun spun through the blinds above the door. Ma was sitting on the rocking chair, the one she bought after winning on the bingo. She was placing towels in a bag to her side. It was the summer time. And it was during those summer years that people from the neighbourhood would hire buses that would take us to the beach. The whole neighbourhood would travel together, with bags filled with sandwiches, towels, buckets, and spades. Ma was gathering all the essentials together.

After breakfast I walked out the front door, sat on the wall and watched the neighbourhood pour out onto the streets. Then the buses pulled in. They belonged to CIE. But they had the names of our roads on the front of them. When the bus was full, a cry went up, the engine started and off we went

Toma, Joe, Weller, and I sat at the back. Goatee was hand-cuffed to his ma. Pat was sitting on ma's lap. Toma lifted up his knee and showed us his scab. He said the sun would burn it off.

"No it won't, the sun doesn't burn off scabs, it burns off eyes if yah stare long enough," Weller said. "I read all about it in a magazine."

"Well I can stare at the sun forever and it won't burn my eyes off," I replied.

"Have a go," Joe said.

"I will."

I lifted my head and stared at the sun as hard as I could. Everything went orange and my head felt hot. So I rested it on the bar in front to cool me down. I wanted to look again. But I couldn't because even with my eyes closed everything was still orange.

"Is he all right?" a woman nodded to ma.

"Are yah all right George?" ma said.

"What's up with him now?" I heard da say.

"I'm alright da," I muttered under my breath. The woman in front told me not to look at the sun with my eyes. Toma said she said that because she looks at everything with her nose; well that's what his da told his ma.

The bus pulled up beside the seafront and all the kids tumbled out the door.

"Here, there's Billy Hard Shoulders," Toma shouted as one of our heroes walked past. He was big in build with a high ribcage and dark brown body that was muscular like that of a gymnast. The music that came out of the radio couldn't catch up with this fella. He looked at us then switched his glance to a nice-looking girl who had the longest hair I had ever seen. The sun shone down on his shaven head and it glowed in the sun, while he walked on like a kingdom all to himself.

He smiled at the girl and held her hand, kissing her at the same time. We all jumped back in the trench, laughing and pushing each other at the thought of him kissing a girl.

"Let's go over here and sit down," we heard him say to the girl, who obeyed him, locking her hand in his.

"Let's follow them," Joe said.

His appeal produced an effect because no sooner had his words fallen when we were up on our toes, creeping through the sand. We kept in hot pursuit until we found a hill to hide behind. And there we peered out like an army of trained spies.

We watched them lying down, eyes closed, arm in arm, and there we struck a deal! Whoever was brave enough to drown them with water would get fifty pence off each boy. I agreed to do it. Toma and Pat came back with the buckets of water and off I went towards them.

The sand was hot under my feet as I snuck up on them, and just as I was in firing range, he caught sight of my shadow. I fired the water, dropped the buckets and ran, kicking the sand into their faces, and across the oil-soaked bodies of my neighbours. Not even the sandwiches escaped!

"Georgie Fitzgerald, wait 'till I see your mother," a neighbour roared as I ran past. I laughed so much that I nearly got sick. When the sun was nearly gone, we ran back to our parents with chattering teeth and hungry bellies, and sat and ate sand-filled sandwiches and washed them down with soft drinks. Then we ate ice cream and got headaches and drank more soft drinks until we got pains in our bellys. Weller said that the rich live like that every day, eating ice cream and drinking soft drinks. He said he seen a programme on the telly all about it. I wondered what it would be like to have headaches and pains in your belly forever.

As the day came to an end, we gathered as many winkles as we could for the journey home. The women would start singing at the back of the bus and then everyone would join in.

At night gangs of boys and girls would gather in the backgarden sheds.

It was there we learned about babies.

"They come from flying birds," Joe said.

"The teacher in the school said that he is going to teach us about the birds and the bees," Toma said, his eyes wide open.

"The birds and the bees," Joe said.

"What about the bees and then the birds?" Git said.

"Yeah that's right," Toma said, "but first it's the birds and the bees."

"Can't wait," Pat said.

"You're too young, Pat, you have to be our age."

"Why?" he said, tears rolling down his eyes.

"Because we know things, that's why," I then added.

"Babies come from flying birds, maybe that's why they call it the birds and the bees," Joe said.

"Na, me ma said that a seed is planted. And then you go out one day, look under the tree and there's a baby," Toma added, looking rather chuffed with himself.

"Na, that's not true," Git said. "Babies come from heaven."

"An angel puts them in your ma's belly, gets a giant straw and blows them up, that's how they're fat."

We all marvelled at Git's story and knew for sure he was telling the truth. Toma wondered whether or not to tell his ma the truth.

"No, Toma, it might frighten her, especially when she hears about the straw," we said.

"Right boys, tea time," ma shouted.

"See Pat, it's thanks to you we are being called in," Joe added.

"Don't say anything about the bees," Toma whispered.

ROUND 11

Joe sat back on a hard leather chair in the barber's shop; I sat across from him, and watched his hair fall to the ground. The shop was called the Classic and it was situated on the second floor of a three storey building in Mary Street. We were growing boys but some things didn't change because I heard a hollow laugh, it was Toma. He sat slumped on the sofa with his head shaved looking out the window while he slagged everyone passing.

It was now 1978, and we had accumulated a lot of victories, while tucking a few titles under our belt. Learning rapidly the art of boxing, beating national champions and still we were only novices.

The barber called me. I jumped off the chair, passed my brother and sat in the seat that he left vacant. He wrapped the white sheet around my neck, and then spoke:

"Number two, Georgie?"

"Yeah," I replied.

"Number two for a number one, the champ," he said with a grin.

"Did yeah hear that? Number two for a number one - the champ, that's the title!" I shouted over to the boys who were now both hanging out the window.

The title I was referring to was the prestigious County Dublin

Championships; it was the highest honour a Dublin boy could win. And in that moment in time, our minds and imaginations were engulfed with visions of winning the championship. Both of us were all ready boxing champions but this title carried a different weight.

When the barber had finished, I lifted myself from the seat, paid him, and walked across the floor brushing the loose hair from the back of my neck. I called the boys.

"Come on lets leg it," I said as we descended the narrow stairs. We strolled up along Henry Street with our hands in our pockets, watching everything going on around us.

We spotted a woman looking in the window of Arnotts. She was staring hard into the glass as if she was admiring her own reflection. Her mind was completely oblivious to the sound of the streets, the passers by, and the two boys who were walking toward her.

The taller boy stopped and looked down as if he was having a conversation with his shoe. The other boy pointed with his eyes to the bulging pocket and his pal quickly picked up on the hint. He then gave a quick motion with his hand for his mate to double back.

Reaching forward he gently touched her coat. He moved closer, dipped his hand in, pulled out the purse, and walked speedily up the street. His young accomplice stepped out of a doorway with a paper in his hand. His hair was sticking up on one side as if he had only woken from a deep sleep. The thief stopped in front of him and we watched him slip his friend the purse.

We switched our glance towards the woman. She placed her hand on her coat, a shocked look covering her face. But the shock soon gave way to a sudden upwelling of screaming.

"My purse has been stolen." The nearest women took up the cry: "HER PURSE HAS BEEN STOLEN!!!"

No sooner had the second cry come out when the thief darted up Moore Street. He burst through the crowd throwing a look over his shoulder, while his clever friend stood back reading the newspaper.

As he turned the corner onto Moore Street, we skidded on the same spot like the Keystone cops. A few children ran along the streets beside a woman carrying a baby. And a small kid latched his face onto the empty stall. The butcher ran out and the dealers left their stalls. Word went from the paper boy to the shopkeeper and from the shopkeeper to the barber, who took great delight in joining the stampede with an open blade in his hand.

But the young boy had great speed, reaching a lane off Moore Street before the crowd. A garda spoke into his walkie-talkie. The crowd moved in slowly. Little children peeked out from behind their mothers clothes to catch a glimpse of the thief.

He stopped long enough to catch his breath, the sweat streaming down his face, every nerve pulsating, but no fear - just anger. He stuck his two fingers in the air and slipped away as if he had never been there at all

"Where's Toma?" Joe asked as we pushed through the crowd.

"There he is," I replied as I saw him walking towards us.

"That's yer man Nicky. He lives down the lower end of the South; he has a brother- goes by the name Mousy. Do yah know them?" Toma asked as the three of us walked past the old red brick building, heading out of the cobble streets.

"Yeah they're always in the Stadium watching the boxing. They have an uncle called Paddy the Lip. Now I heard he's off his head, yeah know what I mean," Joe said.

When night came, Joe and I walked around the bedroom, talking about our recent wins and the victories that lay ahead of us. Pat opened the door and came in and the three of us talked while the night escaped us. But it didn't escape da's attention.

"Come on boys, It's getting late. Boxers need their rest," da said with a smile. Shortly afterwards he came in again, moving our clothes around.

"For Pete's sake boys, keep your rooms tidy, your mother has enough to do."

We snapped to attention and jokingly saluted him.

"Boys the weekend is over, school in the morning," he shouted up the stairs."

"Ok Da," we shouted back and then I would kneel at the bed and pray.

"Dear God, help me da, me ma, Joe, Pat, me grannies and grandas in Ballyfermot. Help me punch everyone hard and faster than they punch me." ♪

A blustering wind stirred the small papers. It sent them flying into the air like tiny kites. It was a grey day, one of those days when you'd wish to be home sitting by the fire. We crossed the street and spotted an old man standing outside an old cobbler's shop in Glasnevin. He was wearing an apron that also blew in the wind. A small woman stood beside him talking, and then she hurried across the street. He raised both hands in the air and then pinned them down on his leg, endeavouring to stop the apron from blowing over his head. Another sharp gust of wind worked its way through the lanes; its force nearly blew my cap off.

"Watch yah don't lose your cap," the grey-haired man said gently, as we passed by. He smiled, it was a very friendly smile. He opened his door and invited us in to his world of shoes, glue and leather straps.

"My name is Shay. What's yours?" He said as he worked on an old pair of shoes.

"I'm George, that's Joseph and he's Weller."

Goatee stuck his head in the door wearing his cap backwards.

"Me name is Goatee."

We watched him cut through the leather sheet, working it on to the soles of the shoes. He peeked over the rim of his glasses, it was a cheeky look.

"I'd say you were born young," he said to Weller, while reaching over and touching the tip of my cap.

Shay was tall, of robust build, full-jawed fresh faced for a man of his years. His eyebrows were thick and bushy. And he seemed to be aware of that because he spat on the top of his fingers and smoothed them back every now and again. Then the old cobbler danced a little, holding his fist clenched when he heard that we were boxers. I noticed his boots were old and turned up at the ends. Little pockets of dust rose up from the floor, as we all moved into our boxing stances shadowboxing around the cobbler, who laughed hilariously with us. He sat on a little stool beside the counter in a room that was at one time a parlour. He fixed his eyes on the old dusty light that dangled from the ceiling. I watched him watch a memory as the tiny insect hovered around the light. In that moment he seemed to have lost the sense of time and space, even though he was in the bosom of curious spectators. And then he came back to us.

"Have yah ever read this?" he piped as he pulled open one of his drawers. It was a magazine called 'Boxing News'.

"Yah can buy them in a shop in Finglas village," he said. "Don't forget, if yah want to be a good student yah have to go to a good school," he added.

By the time we'd finished talking and laughing the sun had fallen asleep and the hand on the old clock didn't give us any indication as to how late it was. But we knew it was time to move on, so we threw our bags on our backs, said our goodbyes and rushed out the door.

I looked over my shoulder as we ran and saw the grey haired man walk slowly to the corner. He watched us with a thousand yard stare, adjusting his glasses and narrowing his eyes as if he had trouble seeing. He then raised his hand into the air and waved, while his apron blew furiously about him.

The rest of the boys sallied along the narrow lane, Weller with his sleeves rolled up, Goatee with his cap tilted back and Joe in the middle. I stopped on the corner and looked up at the black-birds perched across the smoky rooftops. Then I waved and raced after the boys as the cobble streets echoed our departure.

The next day the breeze whistled through the lane in such force it caused the branches to bend over. I pulled my jacket over my head and I made my way towards the bridge.

Shay's words were going over in my mind while I had diminished the distance between my home and the village by cutting through the fields. I had the money in my pocket and I was going to buy the magazine he had told us about.

Suddenly I was approached by a kid from the lower side of the neighbourhood. This type of kid made a career out of bullying smaller, weaker children - and I was a candidate. He was wearing a long black coat and top hat. Apparently wedding clothes had been stolen from a car only a couple of doors from his house! Underneath the hat there was long scraggy shoulder length hair. This kid had bullied us for years. He would take our lunch, kick us, slap us and bite us, while his older brothers ran a protection racket. That was summed up in a few words:

"Pay up and shut up."

The rain began to fall as I approached the bridge.

"Hello there," he muttered, with a smirk on his face. He had a common face, it was the face of a child, but he had the airs and graces of an adult. I gave no response and I tried to pass, but the kid with the top hat was gifted in gaining attention.

He grabbed me by the collar and pulled me closer. He had one hand around my neck, while the other was in my pocket.

"Lost your tongue there Twinny?" he blasted. His eyes were lifeless and ugly.

"Or maybe you're gonna run home and... tell... your... mammy?" he shouted, rolling his eyes towards the sky and tightening his grip.

"Yah want to clean your teeth," I replied sharply.

"Is that right, yah little dope," screamed Top Hat, seizing my coat with great force. He raised his hand and gave me a box. That was followed by another. He quickly became weary from his violent rage. But he tried to drag me along while shouting at me from the top of his voice. I jumped to my feet filled with rage and grabbed him by the throat. I fired a heavy blow. He fell to the ground.

The rain was beginning to get heavier, soaking us through to the skin. Jumping up, he ran at me, but I stood back and caught him with a right upper-cut that put him sitting on his backside. A man jumped out of his car, two women rushed down towards us. My eyes darted around and the little voice spoke:

"Run Georgie - run."

I grabbed my bag, threw it over my shoulder, and ran. The narrow passageways were deep in shadows, I could see boys grappling with one another so I decided to head up the hill and go back across the fields. The earth was slippery with the rain so I moved along by the trees, walking slowly listening to a growing echoing noise.

Someone was running, I heard feet, leather soles crashing off the ground They stopped short. I crouched down and looked out. The drops of rain that fell from the trees washed over me. But my mind was watchful and busy, with all manner of uncertainty that could befall me.

My eyes stretched themselves, falling on the most hideous bunch of youths that anyone wouldn't wish to meet, be it day or night. I heard a police car in the distance, but it was enough to send the prairie dogs running. I slid down the muddy passage back into the lane and then out into the streets and away with me.

When I reached home I sat at the table eating my dinner and listening to ma. She told me to read books, then she told me how important school was, and then she moved on by telling me what happens to boys that get into trouble.

"Once yah get into trouble, yah can never leave the country," she said, "so if you or Joseph ever get into trouble, your boxing is finished."

When I couldn't eat anymore, I left the table, walked to the window and stared out. I felt the heat rise up from the radiator while I watched the rain pelt off the glass.

I noticed a boy running with a face that looked pale and eyes that looked blood shot. He was being chased by an older boy. He fell to the ground. The other boy caught up on him and motioned with his hands for him to stand up. When he didn't, he hauled him from the ground into a standing position. Grasping his throat with one hand, he beat him with all his might with the other. I heard a loud scream and then it got louder, until the kid fell to the ground again. The youth picked him up and shook him violently.

A window opened and a woman stuck her head out and screamed; "Yah dirty scumbag, leave him alone or I'll go out there and smack the face off yah."

Her words reminded me of the woman that roared at my friend Sonny, a week before, only she screamed, "May yah scream for a priest yah brat."

Sonny didn't care what big people said because he stuck his two fingers up as we passed. And then I heard the woman utter: "That boy will die young."

"Right, Pat, put the water on for the bath," ma said.

"George after your bath I'll have a nice apple cake ready."

I smiled. We always smiled when ma made apple cake. We smiled, but ma laughed heartily when she took it of the oven -

her cakes were always shaped like some type of hat!

But as I continued to stare at the little boy crying, I didn't feel much like laughing. Two worlds: one had warm fires, apple cakes, and all the mod-cons, the other had violent boys who used bars, hammers, snooker cues, and knives.

The young gentleman walked away leaving the boy lying in the rain like a dead dog. Two worlds: George would live in here, and Twinny, would live out there. Rocky's words sprang to mind: "*Remember kid hit them first, and hit them the hardest because in this world, only the strong survive.*"

ROUND 12

Shay sat on a chair, outside his cobbler shop during that spring evening of 1979. The rows of houses situated beside him, had baskets of flowers hanging down. Shay was wearing a short sleeved shirt; his hair combed neatly, he had all the hallmarks of a Greek fisherman, sitting on the cobbled streets.

"How's it going boys?" he called, looking over the rim of his glasses.

"Hello Shay," we replied, like little boys visiting their grand-dad.

We launched into our usual banter of jokes and stories, while Weller lit a cigarette and blew rings of smoke into the sky.

The old man peered over the rim of his glasses once again with a concerned look.

"That's not good for you," he remarked in a more sombre tone.

"Yeah, I know that," Weller replied, staring at the ground.

Shay nudged me with a look of compassion and then whispered:

"I read the paper yesterday lads. In it was a story of a boy who achieved great academicals. See if you want to be a good student, you have to go to a good school."

His talk turned to the 1916 Rising and the War of Independence. Then he told us a long story about Michael

Collins and how he saved Ireland against dreadful odds. I imagined I was Michael Collins. I could see myself running through the streets of Dublin saving Ireland while everyone called me a hero.

I glanced at my image in the window and wondered if I looked like him, even though I had no idea what he looked like.

"There are some situations in life that acquire value and dignity that are not always connected to the clothes you wear," Shay expounded, turning towards a small olive-faced woman, as she approached him.

She had a long dress with short sleeves and light brown sandals. In her hand, was a pair of black leather shoes.

"Hello Shay, sorry for coming in so late," she said in a soft, well-spoken accent. "Could you mend these shoes for me please?"

He gazed at the woman as if he was astonished by her presence.

"Of course I will," he replied, tipping the woman's hand gently pointing her to a little wooden chair.

"Oh are these the boys, you're always talking about, the boxers?"

"Yeah, these are the boxers." His smile showed a hint of pride.

"That's George and that's Joe and the other boy is also called Joe, but the boys refer to him as Weller," he then added, pointing at us individually.

He walked inside and began to mend the shoes, talking to the old lady as he worked.

"We'll see you on Wednesday, Shay," we shouted.

"Ok lads, be good now, and remember what I told you."

"We will, Shay," we shouted back as we hurried down the street.

When we got to the club I thought about the cobbler's words. I couldn't grasp the meaning behind them, and wondered about

the word 'academicals'. We discussed it on the way home.
Weller said it was a medal you got when you became a doctor.
But we soon brushed that conversation aside and began dis-
cussing our plans for the County Dublin championships.

The lanes were narrow, the walls were built in old stone.
Leaning over one of them was a large apple tree. I jumped up,
tossed a few apples into my hat and threw some down to the
boys. We ate to our hearts content, caught the bus, and went
home.

♪

We trudged up along the narrow lane at seven o'clock the next
morning. The steel door, at the side of the Stadium was opened
so in we walked, entering into a maze of bodies. This was the
morning we were going to be weighed for the County Dublin
Championships.

Outside, the heavens opened. The hailstones sounded like
rocks hitting off the tin roof. Inside the National Stadium, there
were two weighing scales, one was set beside the ring; the other
stood over at the far wall. Beside them was a table piled high
with loose paperwork, where two men sat checking everything
and everybody.

In front of the scales there was a line of boys, most of whom
looked like they were about to be stamped into a concentration
camp. They were thin, all knees and Adams apples and dressed
in underpants that looked liked nappies.

My name was called. I stepped on the scales, it was cold, and I
was starving. Weight loss is part and parcel of the fight game.
It's the most demanding of all the requirements inflicted on the
human body in preparation for a fight.

A flat-nosed ex-boxer stood in front of me. He was dressed in
a polka-dot jacket, and cream polo neck. He examined the scales
with great intensity. He nodded to me, which I understood it to
mean "take your vest off", which also meant that there was a

problem with my weight. The lines that ran down the centre of my chest were sharp and my mid-section was cut in perfectly, so if I was to shed a few pounds, there wasn't much to shed.

The gangster-looking man turned his head and whispered something to the man at the desk. He waited. I fidgeted. Then he walked around, lifting my chin, so that I felt like I was about to be entered into the 3.45 at Cheltenham.

"Right Georgie, off the scales, you made six stone."

My twin brother made the same weight.

I walked past other boys, wrapped in shabby towels, standing against the wall. An elderly, authoritive-looking man walked towards the scales, dressed in a white shirt and black trousers. He seemed to be dividing his attention between the boys at the wall, and Joseph and myself. His name was Luggs Brannigan or Jim as he liked to be called.

James, Luggs Brannigan was the most famous policeman ever to walk the streets of Dublin. He was a legend in his own time, being chiefly responsible for plundering the criminal world of his day.

He was a frequent visitor to the tenements. In the 1950s, he became famous because of the rough-and-ready trade of street fighting. Stories handed down to us, told of the methods he used. If he believed that a good hiding would be better for you than the courts, you got a good hiding.

Despite his age I could see a young man hidden behind the old skin. He was lean and strong looking with a long face and a head that was capped in grey hair. In my minds eye, I could see him in one of those black and white movies walking along the streets of New York.

Rocky sat on a bench with his head bent over and appeared to be somewhat worried. But he stood up when Luggs approached him. He mumbled something and Mr Brannigan appeared stunned.

"Surely yah explained it to the man," Mr Brannigan said.

"Yeah I did, on cross-examination, but they just aren't listening," Rocky replied.

Mr Brannigan rested his hands on his hips while he listened intently to every word.

"Right Jim, the heel of the hunt is, Joseph is only a few ounces over the 5 stone 7 class and they've placed him in the 6 stone class with his brother. They won't give him the time to knock off the few ounces."

His stunned expression quickly gave way to an angry one.

"Is that right? Well, we'll see about that, so we will."

And off they marched 'till they reached the table where he placed his hands down firmly. We stood there anxiously; Rocky was silent, Jim was angry, while the men were slumped over looking like lambs.

"It's a remarkable coincidence that the Fitzgerald brothers made the same weight," he blasted, while eyeing the man in the polo neck.

"There'll be no haggling here, Jim. Rules are rules and that's that," the man behind the desk shouted.

"Bah! Tis a fine thing te have rules, but I hope yah live by them yourself. Come on, give the lads a chance."

Before he could utter another word, his name was called.

"Right Rocky, keep me informed," he blasted as he walked off.

The man in the polo neck reached across the pile of papers, lifted up a cup of tea and stared at the table drinking it down at remarkable speed. Our manager stared. The man stared back in a kind of fixed wink, which showed that they were having a slight disagreement.

"You're a very fair man all right," Rocky growled and walked away.

He stopped, took a drag on his smoke, stamped it out, and told us to meet him outside.

When we walked into the lane, he was standing there biting down on his bottom lip, meditating on the whole affair.

"Right boys, there's no deals here; yah just got to give it your best shot and see what happens."

We both nodded.

"Joseph you weighed in at five stone, eight pounds - one pound over the five stone seven divisions. I tried to get them to give yah the time to lose the pound, but they weren't having it."

Again we nodded.

"So boys, yis are going to meet each other in the competition. There's nothing I can do."

He shrugged his shoulders, pulled up the collars of his jacket and cursed under his breath.

"I see what you're saying alright," replied Joe.

"As clear as crystal," I added.

Before we had a chance to say anything else he mumbled:

"Come on I'll give yis a lift into town."

So off we walked down the lane hoping against hope not to be matched against each other in the opening rounds.

The night arrived, we were thankfully not pitted against each other. It was dark, cold, and dismal. Both of us jumped up and down trying to keep warm, not taking much notice of anything around us. Then we advanced across the floor towards the dressing room. Joe undressed quickly. When he was ready to leave he stopped at the door.

"Here George, what was it ma always said?"

"If at first yah don't succeed try and try again," I replied.

"Right! Da said if yah want to be the best, yah have to beat the best. This is our time, our time," he said, winking, before leaving.

I lay down in my silk robe, hands bandaged, and new boxing boots. I stared up at the ceiling, rested my hands over my head and waited, like I did when I was younger. That's the hard part - the waiting.

The hand on the clock moved slowly, tick-tock, tick-tock. I watched it until its face became familiar, like that of friend. A second becoming an hour, an hour becoming a lifetime, while time itself drew out, like a long breath.

I stood up, sat down, and stared, at the clock again. When all the staring was done, I hunched my back against the wall and looked at the other boy who sat across from me. His eyes wandered and then rested on me.

"Here, yah got a bye," a voice roared.

A bye meant that you went through the next round without fighting. My heart skipped a beat. I rose off the bench and then realized he wasn't talking to me. He was talking to the other fella who stood up, smiled, and crossed the floor, tipping my fist as he left.

The boom of a church bell rang in the distance, its hallow sound wafted in the open window. I gazed all around and thought of the boys I had fought in the past. Faces rose up, good- looking faces, haggard faces, they ran across my mind.

My thoughts were interrupted when the door opened. I turned quickly and spotted two boys walking in. It was Nicky, the boy who stole the woman's purse, and his brother Mousey. The sound of the crowd rushed in behind them. I heard the bell and a tremendous roar going up. Then everything went silent when the door slammed shut.

Nicky was dressed in a coat that looked like a dressing gown. He displayed a set of features that in no way let him down when it came to his profession. His older brother was smaller but equally as dangerous looking. They huddled in the corner whispering. Standing so close that anyone would think they were kissing.

I jumped up, placed my cap on, and began to pace up and

down, staring at them through the slant of my eyes.

"Twinny, from the South is it?" Nicky exclaimed as he reached over for my hand.

"Yeah," I replied.

There was a long silence, only the sound of the rain could be heard as it fell along the shutters. Nicky jumped on the table, swinging his feet in and out and spoke in a rough Dublin accent.

"Yah know what Twinny? You're a good fighter. Isn't that right, Mousey?"

"You're a proper scrapper. A proper scrapper," he replied, talking more to the bags under his brother's feet. Nicky lit up a cigarette and passed it to his brother. I hurried a glance over at Mousey and watched him crawl along the floor, pulling at the bags like a reptile.

The door handle jiggled. They turned suddenly and stared at one another. It opened and the light rushed in, a shadow stood at the entrance. It was Rocky.

"Here. Get out of here," he shouted at the boys who glared at him before hurrying past.

"Yah can spot them a mile off Georgie," he shouted.

His presence lifted me and expelled the loneliness.

"Don't hide kid, fight. Who are yah, kid?" he asked.

His words were like a double-edged sword cutting through the darkness.

"George Fitzgerald," I replied.

"Right son, fight like the boy you are now. Not the boy you were. To move towards your future, you must forget your past, box on son, box on."

I began to throw punches, left, right, left. Right hand to the body, left hook to the head as we walked out the door.

Danny was standing ring-side watching Joseph's hand being raised. The old man looked at Rocky with an expression of joy and remarked.

"One down, one to go."

"Ah," said Rocky, glancing over at the strong-looking boy who was about to enter the ring. "Let's not count our chickens 'till the egg is hatched.'

"I see what yah mean," Danny replied, glancing at the boy climbing through the ropes.

I went up the steps as Joe came down, tipping off each others gloves as we passed.

The bell rang. I ran out of my corner with my black and white boots breezing across the canvas. My opponent stood upright firing left right lefts like bullets from a gun. I shook them off and noticed his guard was down. I dashed in with a left and right hook, stepped back and brought up an uppercut. I missed. He ran towards me throwing wild body shots. I stepped back slicing the top of his head with a right hand. He stood like a statue. Then I unleashed an explosion of head to body shots. He collapsed. The referee began to count. He failed to beat it. Both of us were going into the next round.

Joe was sitting on a little stool at ring-side in the club the night after. Danny was standing above him hanging onto the ropes, while I paced up and down with my hands in my pockets and cap tilted back. Rocky hadn't arrived yet, but we knew he wouldn't be late. Then the key turned, the door opened and in he walked and headed straight for the far wall.

"Which one did you like best, the book or the film?" he asked, taking a deep drag on his smoke. The question puzzled us.

"Is that your idea of a joke?" I asked, sounding annoyed.

He moved towards me and put his hand on my shoulder and smiled, it was a cheeky smile. I looked at the floor. He repeated the question, placing his other hand on my other shoulder.

"What film?" I said angrily, as I pulled away.

"Somebody Up There Likes Me."

Before we could reply, he cut us off.

"Yah have a chance, boys," he said taking another drag on his smoke. Maybe somebody up there likes you two."

"Here Rocky, you seem to be trying very hard to tell us something."

"What is it?" Joe asked rising from the seat.

"Right here it goes boys. The two of you won't meet in the competition at all; yah both have a chance of reaching the finals."

We looked at each other and clapped our hand together.

"So what that means is - if everything goes our way, we'll meet in the final," I said to Joe.

"Get through the next round first boys, and we'll see what happens, that's boxing... that's boxing," Danny said as we all headed out into the night.

We were scheduled to box the night after. We did and we won. We continued our run of success, right up to the semi-finals. But once we reached them, I began to lose focus, growing increasingly weaker, due to the strict diet that I was on.

With only one more fight left, it suddenly seemed like a task beyond my endurance.

When Joe left the dressing room I began to shadow box, throwing left, right, left and right handed upper cuts. Suddenly I felt my temperature drop; a cold rush ran through me. Danny's hand gripped me, steering me towards the wooden bench. He had noticed a slight stumble in my foot work. I sat for a moment with my hands on my head waiting for him to leave. When he did, I kneeled and prayed.

"Dear God I need your help."

It was only a few seconds walk to the ring, but I walked it slowly. I clinched the steel steps, witnessing Joe put on a great show. In the first round, he went out punching like a champion in the making. The crowd roared as he connected with sharp left hands, that was followed by crashing right hooks.

As the round ended, his opponent ripped through his defence, catching him with a powerful left cross. He fell, hit the canvas and grabbed the bottom rope. The referee began to count one, two, three, four. My heart skipped a beat. It looked like it was all over. He stood up on the count of five. The bell went. The round ended and Danny pulled him back into the corner. He was given smelling salts to bring him back from the dead.

When the bell went for the second round my brother charged out of his corner. Rising from the dust of defeat into a fire of glory, he demolished the future international fighter and went through to the finals.

His opponent, Mick O' Brien was one of the toughest and hardest punchers we'd ever come across. In the years to follow he would put many a man to sleep with the rocks he called his fists. He went on to win a couple of Irish titles and box for Ireland.

"Right George there's the steps," Rocky said.

"They're not steps, Rocky - they're mountains."

"It's not the first mountain you've climbed," he said with the side of his mouth.

"Up yah go Georgie boy and bring us back the title."

I stood in the corner with an iron mask of composure on. But I felt that it was cracking and I didn't want the little boy inside to be exposed. I gasped as I received a few thundering left hands to the body and head.

The wind of defeat that was cloaked in discouragement, whipped across me, in a fire of exhaustion. It was a nanosecond of time. A sudden movement in which I dug deep into the earthly crust, into the will and stirred up a spirit of victory.

"Box on," the ref shouted.

I began to move more confidently around the ring flexing my

arms serious and hard. After three gruelling rounds, I took the victory, and went forward into the final.

The newspapers ran two stories about us. One headline went- "Twins reach final stages", while another said "Fitzgerald's through".

♪

It was a night that dreams were made of when a boy's expectations come true. The sun was high on that spring evening; it had made an unexpected appearance, as if to applaud the two young fighters.

The car pulled in, Rocky reached over and opened the door. We stepped in sitting side by side, in our blue velvet jackets, white tee-shirt, and tight hair. It was a night we will never forget.

"Right lads here we go to the National Stadium," he said looking at us through the rear view mirror. The window of the car shuddered from a blast of wind that came from a passing lorry. The inside was filled with the scent of aftershave that could have easily caused an explosion

When we arrived at the Stadium, Danny was waiting outside. He opened our door, while Rocky closed his.

Rocky was dressed in a black leather jacket and cream trousers. He looked rather dignified. He smiled at us. It was a lively, bubbly smile and then he said,

"'Well done, well done boys."

My twin brother and I both reached the final. By right we should have been fighting each other, but our parents wouldn't allow it because they felt it would bring about conflict between us, so we tossed a coin - and I won.

The announcer called us into the ring. We were received by the applause of the onlooking crowd. Everybody went wild. It was a great feeling. His words echoed around the National Boxing Stadium, filling the ears of all the veterans of the ring craft sitting at the ringside. As one old man, put it: "It's the only time I've seen two champions go into the ring and seen two champions come out."

"Here is the Champion of the six stone classes. George Fitzgerald in the blue corner.

"And this year's runner-up is Joseph Fitzgerald."

The crowd began to applaud, until finally we were given a standing ovation. With both our hands raised, we were presented with the trophies. The two little boys who ran scared along the hallways of Ballymun were being honoured with the seal of excellence in the toughest sport in the world. We had done it.

In that small framework of time, we were lords of all the earth, champions of our world, princes of our destiny.

The papers ran another story the following day, April 7, 1979. The headline read: "Brothers meet in the final." It went on to report about our story and also another set of brothers who were in the same predicament. It stated "in both instances the toss of the coin was used and Michael Carruth of Greenhills and George Fitzgerald of Glasnevin called correct".

Michael would in the years to come go on to win a gold medal in the Olympic Games.

ROUND 13

The sun took a break and ran in behind a white cloud as Toma, my brothers, and I sat discussing the night before. It appeared again like a champion charging out in victory. The clouds moved back like loyal subjects that proclaimed the king is coming, the king is coming.

"Here give us your odds?" a little kid shouted from behind a block wall.

"I'll give yah a clatter if yah don't shut-up," Toma shouted back and turned and winked at me.

Joe and Pat headed back to the house to bring our brother Wesley for a walk. Wesley was the newest addition to our family. At the time he was born the television programme, 'Rich Man, Poor Man' was running. We loved the character Wesley, hence the name of our youngest brother.

I leaned up against a street lamp, eating an apple while I watched Toma play ball with a couple of kids. He ran and kicked the ball up the street. My eyes followed the ball. And as they did, they rested on a boy coming towards us on a horse.

He advanced along the road in slow steps. The horse's hooves sounded like empty pots banging off one another.

I crouched on a step and gazed onto the street wondering how the horse became accustomed to the traffic and the noise of the children. Then I wondered how a boy could control such a large beast.

When I looked again I noticed that the boy was surveying me with great interest. So I put on the same attitude of close observation. When our eyes came into contact I recognized him. It was Sonny.

His shirt was open wide. I could see the thick rope he had tucked in his trousers. His hair was cut tight with a calf's lick standing in the front. He also possessed a handsome face that was knitted together with a captivating smile. Although he was a boy of fourteen years he carried the airs and graces of an adult. He smiled; it was a telling smile, one that had a story behind it.

"Here give us your hand?" he said, while leaning across the horse.

"Na, Sonny, me ma's not into me riding on horses bare back around the streets.

"I'm a boxer, not a jockey," I replied.

"Come on, I have something to tell yah. Go down the end of the road and I'll meet yah there," he said while pointing to the far corner.

"Ok. Here Toma, I'll catch yah later," I shouted as I ran towards the corner.

I climbed onto the horse's back, it gave out a cry and lifted its front feet and thundered across the earth.

We reached the river. I spotted Goatee in the distance, pulling off his clothes and tossing them across the river bank. He waded in, dipped under and came up splashing with his belly shining and then disappeared under again. I wondered what story he was telling the fish.

"Keep your head down," Sonny shouted as we charged past the overhanging trees, wild bushes, and hawks' nests.

I bent forward and glanced towards the sky. I saw two birds fighting. A wailing sound came from them, piercing my ears.

They climbed higher and higher, then swooped and within moments they were charging towards us at great speed. The horse galloped. The winged creatures advanced. We ducked and they cut through the wild overgrowth and landed on a branch.

We ran. "Take a look at them," I shouted, pointing at the frogs in the distance.

Sonny pushed his fingers through the mane and pulled the horse's neck back. It stopped dead. He jumped off and ran like Tonto over to where the frogs were. I could see him crawling through the wild grass like a fox, until he vanished and all I could see was the slight rustling of the grass.

I could hear boys talking, horses hooves clamouring and the bushes breaking. A boy appeared and then another, until I was surrounded by dark glaring eyes. Another boy climbed the hill riding a black mare. He had long hair, high check bones, and a fresh mark above one of his eyes.

"Who owns the horse?" asked the long-haired boy in a raucous voice who went by the name of Johnny B Good.

His jolly friends found the question he asked funny because they fell around laughing.

"Here Charlie, pull Skinhead off the horse," the raucous voice shouted again.

Before they had a chance their horses suddenly went out of control. The boys ran in every direction, waving them down. But the horses kicked and rushed toward them. One of them pulled the makeshift bridle, wrenching it forward. The black mare kicked, missing the handler but catching another boy on the shoulder.

I turned quickly and spotted Sonny standing in the grass with a high-powered sling in his hand, marbles flying everywhere. I pulled the horse's neck around and shot across the field.

"Move over," Sonny roared as he ran alongside the horse.

He jumped up, nearly knocking me off and we charged across

the open fields, heading for the trees.

We went down the steep hill and crossed the river. It was shallow, but the horse struggled climbing the slippery bank. Sonny helped it along with a few encouraging words. And we made it safely across. We rested on the grass with the river in front of us.

"I won the Dublin title last night, Sonny."

"Yeah, I was wondering what that bruise was all about," he said.

"Here wait until yah hear this. Do yah know me brother Sal?"

"Yeah."

"Well, he was coming home from the shops when that cabbage back there catches him!" He took his money and gave him a few slaps. So I don't know this, when I bump into the cabbage, and he starts looking me over, see. So I'm wondering, what's that all about?

"Anyway I get home and there's Sal all messed up, he's crying, there's blood on the floor and me ma's there cleaning him up.

"Then she screams at me, 'I hope this has nothing to do with you'. So I slam the door and walk out.

"I get to work out things in me head. So that night I go down to the fields. I'm standing on the hill at the mouth of the river. This way I can see him coming or going. And right enough he's there, with a few blokes, they're drinking, and stuff. He sees me."

"Here Sonny how did yah know it was him?" I asked, cutting in on his story.

"Sal roared his name as I walked out the door."

"Anyway this bloke gets up and comes over to me. He's a small guy, with a scar over one of his eyes. He goes by the name of Peter the Butcher Boy cos he worked in a butcher's or something before. Do yah know him?"

"Yeah I know him to see."

"Right, he's another cabbage." He started explaining things, saying that Johnny made a mistake, and that he'll sort it out when he sees Sal. So I better forget everything. There were too many of them anyway, so I walked away."

"A few days later I'm walking across the fields in front of me house. I spot these two blokes coming in my direction. I turn around and begin to walk fast. They're walking fast. I'm running, they're running."

"What happened?" I said, not feeling the best for hearing the story, but I wanted to hear the rest.

"Well, I jumped on to the back of the bus and then jumped off in the South; I ran in through the backs and away with me."

By this point the thoughts of last nights victory vanished and I was beginning to feel a little worried for Sonny. It wasn't so much his words that alarmed me or his story. But it was the heart behind it that gave me the most concern. There wasn't too much I could add so after a few minutes silence, we left and headed home.

We followed the dirt road that ran along the river. It narrowed at the end so that's where we crossed. The sky was closed up in a beautiful blue sheet, not a cloud to be seen. We passed trees and hills and heard the frogs again jumping up and down in the long grass. A sea of birds flew between the trees.

I saw three sets of eyes like tiny jewels peering down from behind the thick branches. My mouth flashed open as I stared up. Then I heard a cracking sound. I saw a branch fall and then a body. I jumped off the horse and ran across the grass. Lying on the road like a dead man was my brother Joseph. I rushed over to where he was. His eyes were closed and a small trickle of blood was running down the side of his face.

The branches made a rattling sound behind me. Toma and Weller climbed down. Pat came crawling out from behind the bushes. They ran over, shocked, looking to where Joe was lying.

We lifted him to his feet, he looked weary and crushed, but he was ok. They had been hiding in the trees, ready to ambush us but their plan failed.

Sonny said goodbye, and galloped off across the wild open fields, leaving a trail of dust behind him.

We sat back against the tree trunks. The large silver beams of light broke through the branches lighting up the hard earth that was alive with insects crawling between the wild flowers.

We watched the birds fly into the beams of light, and then they spread their wings and flew out into the open sky. In the distance a cloud of dust was rising and behind it an army of boys.

"Right boys, let's move like shadows" I said, while getting to my feet. "Toma you go ahead in case we get caught, you can get help."

"That's if it comes to that," he replied.

We rushed across the open fields under the hot sun. Toma ran so fast with the gang chasing after him. But to his good fortune he got away and so did we.

Later that evening I cycled around on a big black bike. It was an old war-horse. But it had a special place in my heart because it was given to me by my Granda Stafford. Night was coming and the sound of music filled the streets. The square at the bottom of our road was a meeting place for us. Boys and girls were spread out, listening to the latest sounds of the '70s. *I Want You Back* were the words that filled my ear as I jumped off the bike. Everyone was dressed in the fashions of the day - jeans turned up and Doc Martin boots. The girls were dressed in tight jeans and white runners.

Margo was standing with her back against the wall. She stared at me for a long moment and then smiled. Goatee was standing beside her with a black eye, it wasn't from boxing! His ma had caught him smoking and smacked him so hard that he hit his face off the door.

"Yah want to learn to duck," I said, resting my bike against the wall.

He never replied; he just stood there smoking.

We sat quietly for a while listening to the music. A flat, damp breeze blew across us. It was like an ocean breeze that left a lingering scent in the air, telling us that summer was coming.

"Come on lets get out of here," I said as I stood to my feet pulling the bike upright. I lifted her up on the crossbar, at the same time adjusting the saddle making sure I was balanced right for carrying her. Her black hair swept across my face as we raced in the wind. When we reached her road we walked a while. I could tell by her silence that our courtship was over. I shivered in the cold as the night told me it was time to go.

"So it's over," I stuttered.

She glanced up, looking surprised. I stared at her. She stared back and nodded.

"You're never here. I don't see yah much," she whispered.

I knew in my heart she had found someone else so there was no point trying to win her back.

We embraced and then I cycled home.

Sleep brushed my eyes while I sat in the armchair watching television. So I lifted my body and went to bed. I lay there wondering about the stars. If you could count them, what would their number be? Who calls the north wind out from its storehouse and who awakens the morning? My eyelashes gently met each other as the heaviness of the day clouded me, and I fell into the land of nod.

"It's a heatwave out there," Joe said, as we walked along the corridor in school. A few months had passed since I had won the title and I was looking forward to getting back into the ring. We were both scheduled to box in a club on the docks the following Friday. We talked about this while we headed for the yard.

I bent down to tie my lace. It was then I overheard two boys talking. The information was fragmented.

"Your man Sonny, he's a marked man," the taller boy said as they both rested their elbows on the window sill.

I kept my head low trying to gather as much information as I could.

"Yeah, Johnny said, that Sonny lashed him out of it in the fields with a sling full of marbles. He said the yard is a good spot, plenty of people around, so he can disappear into the crowd."

That was all I needed to hear. I jumped up and walked quickly catching up on my brother.

The schoolyard was situated in the centre of four large buildings which surrounded it. Joe was right, there was scarcely a breath of air, and not a cloud to be seen.

Gangs of youths huddled together. They wore leather jackets, denim jackets, skinheads, and Doc Martins. The formation of these gangs all depended on your geographical location. Gangs from the South hung together, as did the boys from the West, and a small number from the East. But even in the West the gangs were separated. The 'Barry Boys' from the 'Cappagh Boys'. That would be followed years later by 'Cappagh Bulldogs'. In the South a smaller gang was emerging, which called themselves 'The Dirty Dozen'. They will grow and change their name to 'The Filthy Fifty'. Other gangs would rise that will be responsible for the riots that made the headlines in the late Seventies.

Sonny was leaning up against the iron fence, when two boys dressed in denim jeans and matching jackets walked across the crowded yard under the command of Johnny B Good.

They looked at Sonny as they passed and one of them pulled a small bar out from underneath his jacket. Joe and I were about twenty yards away, but we spotted the bar. "Watch your back Sonny," we shouted.

The boy swung the pole, sending it smashing against the fence. Cries and shouts rose up from the crowd, as the boy with the bar staggered and lost his balance.

Sonny moved with great swiftness, firing in a fast flurry of punches. Just then Johnny B Good came walking toward them with a club tightly gripped in his hand, but in the midst of his fury, he was forced to retreat by the presence of the teachers.

The bloody attempt failed. The yard became an angry and tense place. But Sonny with his stealthy feet and watchful eyes disappeared into the crowd and everything went quiet again.

A chill damp wind suddenly blew upon us without any warning. Sonny appeared, dropped his head, pulled up the collars of his jacket so that the bottom of his face was hidden. Then his eyes began to work themselves into a frenzied stare. They moved around the crowd, and then fastened themselves on the two boys that were now weaving in and out between mobs of anxious faces. Johnny B Good was nowhere to be seen.

I threw my eyes over him and watched him change from a boy to a gangster. His mind was evidently wandering, skimming. He continued to mutter, then his voice raised itself above the humming crowds. He motioned with his hands for two other boys to draw near.

They rose from the ground, dusted themselves down, and began to walk towards us. One of them, the taller took the lead, his movements were strange. He took a few steps, looked over his shoulder and looked over his shoulder again. He then took another few steps and moved on. I noticed a small light scar running across the bridge of his nose.

"Here Sonny, see yah have a bit of bother," he observed

through the side of his mouth. The other one eyed Joe and me.

"Na, no bother, yah know what I mean."

"Just find out who them pair of cabbages are, Slipper Boy."

Nobody spoke. So while everyone was saying nothing, both of them lit up cigarettes.

"Here do yah want us to have a word with the bloke we do a bit of work for," Pete said.

"Yeah, his name is Paddy the Lip," Slipper Boy added.

The boy that addressed Sonny was one of the roughest boys we had ever seen. He had a snub nose, sleepy eye, and a flat face. He walked up and down eyeing Joe and me. But we remained hard-faced, shoulders held back.

He reached out his hand.

"Me name is Dan but otherwise known to me mates as Slipper Boy. I got the name for crawling gaffs, yah know what I mean."

In other words he robbed houses when people were asleep.

"Yeah," we replied while we shook hands.

He then turned to Sonny and said: "Don't forget, Paddy the Lip will sort it, if yah want us to have a yap with him."

"Na, I'll sort it Slipper."

"Ok. Catch yah later," he replied as the three of them clapped hands like the Three Musketeers.

When the bell rang for school to end, Joe, Sonny and I walked out onto the porch. Our blood froze when we saw what was in front of us. It was gang of youths holding bars and baseball bats. But we watched Johnny B Good; he was crouched down with his hand in front of him as if he was warming himself at a fire. He was still holding onto a grudge over the incident in the fields.

We took a few steps back and disappeared into the crowd. We crouched like men carrying bundles on their backs, glancing back as we crept up along the wall. The gang hadn't moved. They kept their eyes fixed on the door and we thought we were safe, until a kid that had nothing to do with anything pointed us out.

"There they are," he shouted pointing towards us.

Word ran from tongue to tongue as cries and shrieks came out like venom from their leader.

"Run for it boys," Sonny shouted. We didn't wait around to see if he was joking. There was panting and pushing, striving and crushing sounds rising up into the air, as we ran along the ground, to the point that the earth nearly shook.

I glanced over my shoulder at the maddened faces. There was a wall in front of us, but Sonny saw it as the only possible escape route. So with one leap he cleared it. Joseph ran with no less rapidity but made it over the side - only with great effort.

"Run George," the boys shouted.

"What do yah think I'm doing?" I panted as the tightness pulled on my calf.

The gang was gaining ground. The wall was still a distance from me. I'd suffered a pulled muscle in a work-out and now it was playing up. But I encouraged my feet and kept going. Sonny stretched out his hand.

"Come on George," he shouted. I leapt into the air. It was my one shot, a one way ticket, no return. I kicked my feet trying to get a grip on the wall. The wind caught my jacket blowing it over my head. But I saw a hand reach down, it was Sonny's hand.

A bunch of hands grappled at the back of my jacket. Joe looked fearful. But I caught the hand and Sonny pulled me up over the wall. We raced across the open spaces and headed for a hill of earth and made it over to the other side. I circled along the outside and lay down on the ledge. Sonny picked out a few stones and pulled out his sling. It was a poor plan but it was all we had.

We crawled out and watched them roaming through the open spaces. I saw Johnny B Good looking all around him. His face appeared anxious.

"Let's get out of here," Joe said in a near whisper.

So we moved back and then slowly declined along the steep hill until we reached level ground. We moved as fast as we could, walking a few steps and running a few steps. We stayed together taking a short cut through the houses until we came to a few steps that lead into the South. There we let out a sigh of relief.

"Thanks Sonny," I said.

"For what? Yah didn't think I'd leave yah there, did yah?"

His words sounded like an old song. We all laughed.

The story ended for Joe and myself once we reached our street, but Sonny wasn't about to let the boy with the black hair away. As the story goes, the one we heard later, Sonny was consoling himself with thoughts of revenge, planning it out to minute detail.

He sat around waiting for his opening. It came on a cold rainy day in May. The boy in question was walking towards the school. Sonny appeared from behind a doorway. A small ball went into the air. The boy lifted his head and followed it. What he didn't see was the old car exhaust that went crashing against his head and arms. Sonny beat him with great force. The boy went staggering across the main road with a deep gash across his forearm. Onlookers ran across the street. Sonny stood over him, seizing the weapon one last time, and striking it down on him.

Johnny B Good suffered two black eyes. Sonny was on the move. But one of those moves turned out to be near fatal. Not for him, but for a woman, who happened to be in the wrong place at the wrong time.

You see, to Sonny the world had no rules, no laws, and no boundaries. If you needed something and it wasn't nailed down, you just grabbed it - that was his philosophy.

Anto his mate shared the same mindset. He was a lean boy

with narrow shoulders, a boy that looked like he was reared on gruel. His face was pale and his hair was cut short at the back and parted in the centre. His dream in life was to raise better thieves than himself!

Two teenagers entered a shop wearing balaclavas and carrying a shotgun. One of them glanced out the window and saw a police car crawling up the street. The young mothers picked up their babies and screamed.

"Just gives us the money from the till," Anto roared. Here, Sonny, Sonny, grab the cash."

"Leave it. Here's the law."

They made a run for it. The car went out of control, hitting the path and knocking a woman to the ground. The woman was lying under the car. Anto was about to drive on. But Sonny pulled up the handbrake, jumped out and picked the woman up. Thankful she was ok.

They drove off, hitting about seventy miles an hour. They saw another police car coming toward them. They drove across the fields and headed for the South, into a narrow lane, blocking the entrance. There was a fence in front of them, Sonny cut through it. By the time the police arrived, all that was left was a blazing car.

They rushed along the streets, dived into a backyard and crouched down with flies buzzing around. Anto cocked the shotgun and pointed it into the air, just in case a Garda came over the wall. The rain began to fall, small drops at first then large ones that were more consistant.

They heard a whistle, it was silent and dry. Sonny looked at the door and seen a bulk of a boy standing there.

"This way," the bulky kid said, walking indoors.

They followed him past the old fridge and the broken television. Their nostrils being assaulted with the smell of fish and rubbish over flowing from a neighbours bin. A car pulls in, the doors open, the boys jump in while the gun is whisked away.

Sonny looked like his father, a big man who wore monkey hats and caps and never drank or smoked. He worked on the docks and reared his family to be honest. His mother was a small woman who hated the sight of trouble, a hardworking mother, with thirteen children to look after.

Sonny was stealing from an early age. His first recollection of stealing was at the age of five, when he stole a few pencils in school. And by the time he was ten he was making good money selling anything from toilet rolls to vegetables, either on the streets or door-to-door.

At night he slept in the same bedroom as his six brothers. The only heat they had was a coal fire in the sittingroom. There were only three bedrooms, one bath, one toilet.

In the winter, coats were used to keep warm. He would often bring home coal or wood for the fire, but his father would run him at the first sign of anything that was stolen. But one thing that Sonny had going for him was that his father and mother never gave up on him. And for this wayward boy that was a good thing because the path he took and the places he was going not many people would stand up for him.

ROUND 14

Joe and I left the house and headed to the village. The buses had stopped coming through our area; it was a temporary situation that happened from time to time. It was six o' clock, we knew that because we could hear the Angelus ringing from a television in a nearby house.

Micko a neighbour, who was standing on the corner, shouted over to us: "Here Twinny, did yah hear the news about Marko? He got an L-plate."

An L-plate was a life sentence.

"Yeah," we shouted back in unison. And Joe quickly suggested: "He'll probably end up getting one as well."

It was a nice evening and the club didn't open until seven so we had plenty of time. We decided to cut through Finglas South and catch a bus at Premier Dairies. A bus passed, we missed it, but we saw Sonny running up the hill towards the old house on an estate in Finglas East.

"Come on," Joe said. "Let's see what he's up too." We'd no sooner reached the corner when we saw Sonny creeping in through the front door of the old derelict house. Joe and I stopped for a minute to catch our breath and then followed him into the house. Joe was holding his mouth and I was holding my nose, both of us trying desperately not to laugh.

The stairs in the old house consisted of about seven steps

between floors. The first landing was lodged between an arch and a wall; it was a perfect hiding place. We stepped in and watched Sonny grope the dark walls with one hand while he held the other hand in front of him, climbing each step with the greatest of care. When he got to the first landing he looked all around and walked up the next flight of steps. We walked into the exact room on the landing below. The walls were coated in age with names written all over them. There was a deal-table, an old fire place and a candle stuck in a wine bottle. We could hear Sonny cross the floor and flick his lighter to light a cigarette.

"What's he doing here?" Joe said.

"Why don't yah ask him? Yah might as well. He's probably after hearing yah anyway," I whispered.

While he sat and smoked, wondering to himself inside, two youths stood outside, glancing all around them. Joe and I could see them from the window. When the coast looked clear, they carried their long boney bodies and their hard features, up the pathway and in through the open door, along the same steps that we had taken a few moments earlier.

The larger youth walked in looking over his shoulder, moving on and then looking over his shoulder again.

"I wished ya'd picked a better place," he roared from the door of a room on the same floor as Sonny. The empty house carried their voices down along the staircase as if they were spoken through a loud speaker.

"Why's that, scared of ghosts?" We heard the voice of Johnny B Good say.

The three young gentlemen laughed hilariously at Johnny's notion that they could be scared at all, ghosts, or no ghosts.

"Sonny wanted to know, who the blokes were that yah set against him, and if I was you, I'd watch yer back," the sly Slipper boy said.

I looked at Joe and nodded at him to go.

Johnny, got up off the chair and began to pace around the room. We heard a loud noise, like a chair being kicked.

"How are we going to get out of here, George?"

You're the one who brought us in here in the first place. Where's Sonny?"

"Do yah want one?" Johnny asked Slipper and his mate Pete.

"Do yah want a smoke, or what?" he asked for the second time.

"Yeah go on, nice one Johnny," Slipper said. He seemed nervous.

"No problem," Johnny replied.

"Lets get out of here," Joe whispered.

I took the first few steps, Joe came behind me.

"That Sonny fella's days are numbered," we heard Johnny mutter as he banged down on the table.

"Keep it down," Pete said softly.

"What did yah say? What did yah say?" Johnny roared.

The room became silent. Johnny must have been reflecting. I reached the door, my eyes bulging; Joe's palms were sweating.

We tip-toed along 'till we reached the landing. We turned our ears to the room and heard Johnny roar.

"Well, we'll just have to sort him out, the way Paddy the Lip told me too."

"How's that?" Pete asked, his voice seemed to tremble.

"Slice him once, slice him more 'till all that's left is the blood on the door."

We jumped down the last few steps and out of the door, running around to the side of the house to where Sonny's room was. We saw his window open and deep footprints in the soft muck. So we disappeared just as the darkness came.

By the time the cold windy days of March had passed it was

time for us to step back into the ring. I paced up and down along the narrow passage behind the seats in the Stadium. Danny filled the bucket with water and carried it down along the aisle. He crouched down at ringside and glanced towards me. I scanned the area in front and looked down at the concrete steps. I heard a quick intake of breath behind me and Rocky spoke.

"The key to victory is not to give in to your emotion."

The Stadium was swarming with people mostly men and boys, sitting, standing, shouting. They crowded the aisles and passage ways that ran behind the seats.

I began to imagine that I was the greatest fighter in the world. I could see myself winning the world title. My thoughts were interrupted by a harsh Dublin voice:

"That kid you're up against will beat yah. He's a great scrapper."

On hearing those words I turned quickly. Behind me was a small obese shaven-headed man. He had a glass eye, a broken nose, and a cripple foot.

In the distance I could hear slaps and blows, the roar of the crowd and the cries of kids struggling to see the fight. A gang of men descended the stairs wearing donkey jackets and smoking cigars. They called to the fat man.

"I'll be there in a minute," he roared.

I leaned forward and spoke lowly: "You're a nosy oul fella that should mind his own business."

I walked down the aisle and entered the ring.

The referee crossed the canvas, checked my gloves, lifted my chin, and stared into my eyes. Then he walked away. As he did, I caught sight of my opponent climbing through the ropes. He was wearing a hooded top that reached down to his boxing boots, and when his trainer removed it, a tank was standing in front of me with a shaven head. This boy had not only won the national title but also received an outstanding award for best boxer in the country.

"Breathe slowly," Danny said as he glanced at his watch.

I closed my eyes while he placed the mouthpiece between my teeth, then breathed deeply and exhaled slowly. Toma and Joe were sitting at ringside with Rocky.

When the bell rang, we tipped both gloves off each other and I ran out punching as fast as I could. My opponent's gloves made a whistling sound as it crashed against my jaw. My head dropped while my mind descended into a spiral of thoughts that were quickly stepping back into my childhood.

The champion rushed forward carrying his fists like tools that were furnished on the anvil of time and pressure. Instruments of hardness knotted together by a violent but controlled aggression.

I moved back. The crowd groaned. I lifted my head. He was walking towards me. He threw a left hand. I ducked, side-stepped, and brought up a right uppercut and followed it by a double left hook. He trembled; his strong torso and steel arms appeared ridged. He fired over a wild right hand. I stepped inside and pounded his midsection, forcing him back on the ropes. Left, right, left. Right hand to the body, left hook to the head.

The bell rang ending round one, two, and three. And my hand was lifted up and I was declared the winner. Joe won his fight easily too. Both of us boxed our way up towards the final.

On the morning of the final, the newspapers reported two stories. One article read: *Twins through* and the other read: *Twins reaches final stages* . The morning following the final, another article unfortunately read: *Joseph was beaten in a very tough fight. The victory could have gone to either boy. The father of Joe's opponent believed that his son was fortunate to have won, but that's boxing.*

And so it happened that I was, once again, through to the

finals.

♪

"Move, step forward," Rocky shouted.

The light in the dressing room was dim. We exchanged glances; both our eyes seemed to be on fire. This was my big night, the night of the final

The little room was packed. I walked around breathing deeply; dressed in a hooded robe and black boxing boots with my initials printed on the side. My hands were tightly wrapped with new white taped bandages.

"Give me a bit of space, Rock," I groaned.

"Right boys, outside until he's ready," he shouted.

He didn't have to repeat himself.

The old dressing room had a small window, but a thick shadow of light rushed in. That's where I kneeled on the cold dark tiled floor and prayed.

"Dear God give me the courage to fight bravely, please."

After I blessed myself, the door opened.

"You're up next," Rocky said. And then he led the way along the narrow corridor.

A small heavy man wearing a red polo shirt, hurried along the concrete steps, carrying a bucket of blood and water. The crowd roared as the other fight came to an end. I stood for a moment, looking for Joe and the boys, and then I spotted them. Rocky turned towards me in typical fashion and said:

"Right George, go and bring us all back the title. Here kid, when you're in there, I'll say a prayer for a boy who's as tough as nails."

"Thanks Rocky," I replied, looking into the tough man's eyes.

I glanced around the fighter's gallery and noticed Toma waving. The rest of the boys by his side had their eyes on me. But I couldn't busy myself with their attention; I had a job to do.

In the far corner was a red haired lean boy. He was a couple of inches taller than me. He was also three times national champion and he held a tremendous record. Before the bell rang Danny leaned across the ropes and said; "George son, let your gloves decide the winner."

I turned and glanced over the old familiar ropes for Joe. I caught his gaze; his dark grey eyes spoke volumes.

"Go George, win."

The bell rang and I went out punching as hard and as fast as I could, my muscles rippling like the pistons on an engine that was firing on all cylinders. Coming to the close of the second round, the referee commanded me to stop. I had to step back because he gave me a public warning, the implication being that I could lose the round on a technicality.

I won the second round easily, but in the middle of the third round he gave me another public warning. Stepping back in shock I looked to my corner. Rocky looked angry, Danny disappointed.

"Keep focused," he shouted, placing his hands above his mouth; his voice reaching my ears above the roar of the crowd.

I turned my eye upwards; little beads of sweat broke out across my forehead, stinging the cuts above my eyes. My heart was racing. The blood from a cut on my bottom lip filled my mouth.

In that moment everything seemed to move in slow motion, the crowd, Rocky, Danny. I glanced at Danny and gave a deep sigh. Joseph's head was between his hands.

The air was heavy with rising smoke clustering around the bright lights. I raised my head, glanced across at the Irish champion. He was now pacing up and down in his corner like a caged lion.

"Box on," the referee shouted.

I rushed across the ring, pounding left and right hands into the champion's head, sending him crashing onto the ropes. He hung on with his head bent over. I marched forward keeping the politics out, as I carried the unwritten rule into the ring, hit them first, hit them the hardest.

I fired in more punches, each one like a missile, landing at their appointed destination. His face was covered with blood, his eyes about to close when the bell rang. He was out-boxed, out-punched, as one man, put it. It was the bloodiest battle he had witnessed, as the little kid with the skinhead, demolished the champion.

"The winner and County Dublin Champion of the seven stone seven class, in the blue corner, G. Fitzgerald."

Throwing the gloves on to the blue canvas, I ran across ring. The crowd were cheering and rejoicing. There was an old man sitting on the bench. He was so overwhelmed that he jumped off his seat the wrong way and strained his back. I heard later he had to be lifted out.

Jumping up on to the bottom rope I looked for the young boys with the tight haircuts and the caps. They were all dancing, while Joseph stood in the centre, smiling. I showered, dressed, threw my cap on, and met the boys outside before leaving the Stadium.

The once great fighter was now an old man. He was standing with his back against the wall beside the gutter. He had a bottle in his hand and his cap pressed down.

"Here kid, keep going," he roared as we all walked out of the Stadium.

The air was cold, sharp, and the night dark. I turned quickly.

"Keep going," he roared in a heavy Dublin accent. As I turned to walk away, he cursed to himself and called again.

"Are you the champ?"

"I am," I replied.

"Come'ere then."

I walked over slowly. Joe and the boys walked on.

"Yah know wha' kid?"

"Wha'?"

"Don't walk down this alley in life, yah hear me."

"Yeah."

"Good kid. There are too many ghosts here, too many."

He pushed me. I stepped back, and he leaned forward, saliva dripping from his mouth.

"We don't need anymore here. Be a champ in life, in life kid," he roared.

I ran, laughing, tugging at the boys. But I remembered his words, but most of all his eyes because there was a dead man in there.

The bus was packed. I sat alone at the back, the boys sat at the front. Nicky jumped on.

"Here, Twin, yah done good."

"Nice one, Nicky."

He pushed the person who was sitting beside me over and made room for himself.

"Yah know wha'? Me granda was a great scrapper. He came from the cage down on Corporation Street, but they moved up to Sean Mac. That's where I was born."

And while I sat back, he told me his very sad life story. I felt pity for him and his brother and I couldn't wait to tell Joe the story I had heard.

Joe walked into the bedroom and I followed him. Pat and Wesley were asleep. Ma and da were watching the telly. We sat and talked about boxing. Joe interrupted me.

"I'm finished with boxing."

"Wha'! Are yah mad or wha'?"

"Na I have a bird now."

"Yeah, Jackie won't mind."

"Well I was going to tell yah a story about Nicky. I'm not telling yah now."

I slammed the door. Da was standing on the landing. I walked past him. He followed me into my room.

"George, boxing was never me or your mother's choice for yis but, as far as we can see, it's not doing yis any harm. But yah really need to brush up on your school work."

"Yeah, ok, Da, but I am going to be a world champ one day."

"Right but what happens if your not? Do yah want to end up working in a dead-end job?"

I undressed and got into bed.

"Just have a think about it and don't forget to say your prayers," he said before leaving.

ROUND 15

My left hand lead was thrown with lightning speed. But my mind was on Jim Macken and Larry Molloy at ringside. My opponent stepped in and made me pay for my lack of concentration, peppering my head and body with sharp blows. I had fallen into the killzone area. Ten or so shots later the canvas was rushing towards me. Every waking second it drew nearer. I dropped like an apple from a tree

"Get up George," my mind instructed me.

I blinked, looking up at the referee counting one, two, three. Before I knew it he was waving his hands and shouting, "Out!"

I was whisked away and left in the dressing room. Joe was standing in front of me.

"What happened? Did I get stopped?"

"Yeah."

I placed my hands on my head and began to rock to and fro like a baby. My mind was flooded with thoughts, tears streaming down my face.

"I was afraid Joe," I blurbed.

"It's all right, it's all right."

I slowed down, looked at Joe and said, "I was frightened Joe." I was afraid."

The following year, I took the Dublin bantamweight title. The newspaper report said I had overwhelmed my opponent in the final. That was the year I went to the North and beat the Ulster champion. The newspapers said:

"Fitzgerald - a rock has landed." The UTV news reported that we had 'arrived' and the radio covered the fight. But best of all I got to wear an Olympic medal for a few moments.

When I got back to Dublin I trained all summer on my own. And I then crossed the water to England.

There was no covering on the concrete floor in the dressing room. I had to shed a few ounces because I was over the weight. With no windows, it was hard to tell the time. I knew it was late. I hadn't slept on the way over. And I hadn't eaten anything for two days. I was now seventeen-years-old. I jumped rope, shadow-boxed, stepped on the scales, made the weight, seen the doctor, dressed and then walked out.

All around me were men standing on the balconies, on the floor and sitting at tables shouting in English accents. They were watching men beat each other to a bloody pulp.

I crossed the tiled floor, between the rows of seats. The place erupted when the other Irishman was sent flying across the canvas.

"Remember Georgie, fight like an Irishman," the trainer shouted.

The bell rang. I walked out, fixing my glove, and I received a flurry of punches for that mistake. The ropes were burning the back of my neck, the blood sprinkling the canvas. I glanced up and saw eyes coming towards me like lanterns beaming in the darkness.

"Move Georgie," were the shouts I could hear from the corner.

The gentlemen were on their feet as the Irishman was taking a beating.

I sidestepped, catching him with a riveting left hook. Sliding under a barrage of punches, I worked his mid-section. The wind left his body, as he dropped to the canvas the bell rang.

For the next two rounds we stood toe to toe. In the middle of the third round, I felt a cracking sound. My mind rushed back in time. Another punch ripped through the bridge of my nose bringing with it a steady flow of blood.

The referee walked me to my corner. My nose may have been broken, but there was still a flame in my spirit. The coach ran up the steps with a cloth in his hands and a bucket of water by his side.

"Come on Georgie, keep your head back," his words were filled with panic as he plunged the sponge into the blood filled water. He pressed down on my head - until the water trickled along my face, and down along my chest.

Suddenly, I lost the hearing in my left ear.

"Here, I can't hear nothing. I can't hear, me ear is gone all mad," I shouted.

"Hold on son, hold on," the trainer shouted back, pushing my head forward.

"Oh no! Your ear is busted, but don't worry, the referee hasn't copped it."

I leaned back and stared up at the large crystal chandelier that was above me, while the doctors of the ring went to work. The light shone down and the noise rushed around me. I felt my mind drifting.

"Daddy when I gets to be a big boy I'm going to tell s-norys."

"George."

"Yeah, Da."

"Georgie, Georgie are yah still with us? Come on lad, let's get to work, yah can do this."

I stared at him. In my minds eye, I saw a little bushy-haired boy. He was shadowboxing in an old ring. And behind him I saw a tiny boy standing in the corner in school. My eyes were opened but my mind was drifting. No sleep, no water, no food, nose broken, ear busted.

I see the sun and the sand. I am running. It's wonderful. I am given a guided tour of the largest mountains and the clearest blue streams. I am free. A black hand that belonged to a faceless person grabs me, rushing me into the corner.

"Stay there you dunce. You fool. You're never going to amount to anything, bad boy."

"Come on son, fight back."

The penny dropped. The boy in the corner was trying to fight his way out. But in that moment, I knew this wasn't the way.

After I was drowned in a bucket of water, I lifted myself from the stool.

"Box on," the referee shouted.

The war raged on. I stepped back, firing a wild swing with the might of the Irish behind it. He dropped to the canvas. I fell, holding myself up while resting one hand on the top rope.

The final bell rang and my hand was raised in victory on English soil on the March 17 - Paddy's day!

"You're all right, Paddy," the English fighter cracked.

I glanced over my shoulder and muttered back: "That's me granda's name."

He smiled, all bruised and battered looking. He took off his glove, reached out his hand and shook mine. We both had won each other's respect in the gladiator arena.

That night I inserted the key into the door of the hotel room. I stepped into a shadowy room and sat on the bed. It was here I experienced an overwhelming sense of regret and questioned why I ever boxed at all.

I groped the wall looking for the switch. I found it and snapped it down. I moved forward to the window. Thrown off-balance by this unfamiliar feeling, I stared out at the blackened sky and the rough sea.

I lay on the bed and thought about what it would be like to have a girlfriend and wondered if there was anyone out there for me, and if there was, what was she doing? I slept peaceful.

My father George Fitzgerald snr pictured on the left before I was born. And the above picture is of him today

Joseph and I in Ballyfermot circa 1965 and the right is our communion day, 1970

To catch a pearl...Sandra and I on our wedding day, 1990

The above picture was the cover for our top 10 single "People Lets Dance". Below is the cover of our first single 'I Surrender'

left to right, Pat, me and Joe in Ballymun circa 1969

Daniel and Nathan today

Sandra pictured during band shoots and play-ing with the D-11 Runners playing a con-cert in Browne Thomas.

Me today.   *Pic by Jason O'Toole*

The pictures on the left are of Joe, Paulo and me, after I won the County Dublin Championship. The above photo is of me in the UK. The picture below is of Joe and me.

The Fitzgerald brothers in Finglas South.

My mother Marie and Sandra. The middle picture shows me and my son Nathan as a baby, and the picture on the right is me and my son Daniel as a baby

The next morning I jumped up, took a shower and went down for breakfast. Afterwards I decided to go for a walk.

The hotel was set on the seafront, so that's where I headed. The sea was flat and calm as I strolled quietly along the beach, throwing small pebbles into the water.

"The currents here can be dangerous," an old man said as he passed by.

"Yeah thanks," I shouted back pulling my cap down as I walked out onto the pier.

The long narrow pier opened up in a square. I hung over the white railings, the wind blowing in my face. That's where I made up my mind, I was finished boxing.

On the way home I sat on the boat and listened to men singing an Irish song, but I couldn't wait to get home and run away from Irish songs, the ring, punch bags and strict diets.

I stepped off the boat, dodging between the crowds. The horn on the bus sounded. I turned and waved as a few cheers came from the boxers hanging out of the windows. The docks were paved in human faces but it was Rock's face that nearly brought a tear, as he waited at the dock.

"Good boy, son. Hey look, you're a man now," he said smiling.

I placed my bag down and tilted my hat backwards.

"Rocky, I'm finished. I'll never step into the ring again. I've had enough."

He never protested, he just simply looked at me and shook his head slightly.

The sky above us seemed to be on fire. And in the distance a bell was sounding, calling people to board the ship. Few words passed between us. He then took a drag on his smoke and said

"That's that. Right son, come on I'll drop yah into town. Yah need to get that ear looked at."

"Na it's all right Rock, I have to meet a mate," I lied. I didn't want to sit and talk boxing. I just wanted to run.

"Right son, he said, talk to yah soon."

He reached out his big hand and we said our goodbyes. As I walked off he shouted, "Here George, I'll say a prayer for a kid who was as tough as nails."

I placed my bag on the ground and waved, he waved back at me, watching me through the rear view mirror.

I never did see the tough inner city man again. A drug addict struck him across the head as he tried to defend his property. He was murdered on the streets of Dublin. Danny will die the way he lived, alone in some nursing home. I heard at the end, he died in the arms of his only brother.

Goodbye Danny. Goodbye Rocky. I was a little boy who was afraid to fight, but you both seen me through, in a world where only the strong survived. Thank you.

When I finally made it to Finglas, I rested my bag on the ground. And thought of all the apple cakes I could now eat. Then I glanced across the countless rooftops wondering what I would do next. But what I wasn't aware of was that a few blocks up, Sonny was running.

I walked on and headed up a lane. So did Sonny. I turned the corner. So did Sonny. I walked through another lane. So did Sonny. I came out. Sonny was caught. A blade went into the air. Sparkling when the sun hit it, a hand gripped it tightly, and then brought it down in great ferocity. The blood splashed off the block walls. I walked up to the door, knocked once, and dropped my bag. It hit the ground hard. So did Sonny.

ROUND 16

By this time I was serving my apprenticeship as a plasterer. The site was across town. There were some very interesting characters.

Tommy's shoulders and wrist were in line with each other as he pulled the plastering trowel across the wall. If trowels had a voice, he was the man who could make them talk. He had a pair of hands that even Michelangelo would have admired. The grey hair that graced his head and the short muscular body he lived in would put you in mind of Jake La Motta, the boxer.

"Here's the muck," Billy Block-Head shouted to Tommy in his wild and boisterous manner. But he didn't hear him. Or he didn't want to; it was one or the other.

In those days plasterers were required to wear white overalls and caps. Tommy and myself were no exception.

I crossed the plank with my hawk full of skimming and handed it over to him. In the background the wheels of the barrow made a squeaking sound, as the men in vests rushed up the plank to empty the rubbish into the shoot. Everywhere the eye travelled there were men carrying blocks, rolling empty barrels, stacking plasterboards, or using kango hammers.

"Right son grab that feather-edge and pull it over the wall."

"Here's the muck Tommy," Billy roared again, holding his hand over his mouth trying to raise his voice above the noise.

Tommy didn't hear him, but I saw a glint in his eye that told me he did.

"Here Tommy, Billy Block Head is looking for yah," I shouted.

"Yeah what's the story with him?"

"Have yah got that muck mixed yet?" Tommy roared, while winking at me.

"Yeah, yeah, relax we'll get it up in a minute," Billy replied. "Oh by the way, Big Ron is downstairs, he's looking for a start. Will I call him up or what?" he then asked, walking away with an attitude that said, stuff the muck.

"Yeah call em up, I have a number for him," Tommy replied.

The floor we worked on was knee-high in old bags of plaster, rubbish, broken blocks and lines of steel that was covered in green scum. Big Ron stepped over them and walked in looking like a rich landlord, dressed in a black jacket and a trilby hat and not forgetting the big moustache, hence the name Big Ron. I liked him because he was not only a great plasterer, but he had been a great boxer in his time. He and Tommy didn't pass many words between them. I could see that their past wasn't exactly a blessed one.

"How's the training going George?" he asked as he placed the number in his top pocket, completely avoiding Billy and Tommy.

"Yeah, it's going well," I lied.

I hadn't the heart to tell him I was finished with boxing.

"See yah got a busted vein."

"Yeah, I had to go under the knife when I got back from England. But the doctor said it won't look too bad when it heals."

"Keep it up son. Yah don't want to stay in these places for the rest of your life, now do yah?"

I just nodded. He left without saying goodbye to the others.

That day I had a heavy debate about boxing, with Billy and a few other men. Billy jumped up out of his chair like a big child and said: "Right Georgie, bring in them boxing gloves tomorrow and we'll see how good yah are," before slamming the door and walking out.

"Georgie give that mouthpiece a good hiding," laughed Git Moore as we headed up Pearse Street that evening.

The following day, I brought in the old pair of boxing gloves after deciding to take on the challenge. There was a lot of back-talk going on and word swept through the site that Billy and I were to face each other in a duel. The sun outside hadn't made any great impact, but it was still very humid.

The horn rang throughout the site, signalling lunchtime. The canteen was placed down along the timber fences. Above it was the foreman's office and about twenty feet away stood the old building we were working on. It was rich in history. The outside was finished in black stone with large arched windows running through it. The inside was equally attractive in its architecture. It was without doubt a building where Dickens famous character, Fagan, would have felt very comfortable, along with his gang of pickpockets.

Half the men followed me, while the other half followed Billy. They raised their shovels above their heads and chanted our names. The dust under their feet rolled up into a scroll as we marched up the hill of bricks, rubble and planks, towards the old eighteenth century house.

Once inside, I pulled my overalls down to my waist and put on my gloves. The old timber floor creaked and the pigeons scattered towards the timber beams when Billy began jumping up and down. Johnny acted as referee. He was a Mayo man and was built like an ox. He was one of those men who I'd say was raised on pots of cabbage. He had the head of a giant and a nose that would make Pinocchio look like an honest puppet!

"Right boys, the first one knocked down will be the loser," Johnny shouted, as the men formed a human ring around us.

Big Davy the old pro was in my corner, with Git Moore by his side. Davy was dressed in this long coat, and curled-up boots. Davy, the coat, and the boots bore all the hallmarks of a character that had jumped out from the pages of *Strumpet City*.

He was a tall man of very muscular build. He wore his broken nose like the way men wore their caps. He said it was a symbol of character, although I had some reservations about that. He also talked like a character from a book and never gave a straight answer - everything was spoken in riddles. He had in the past boxed in England as a pro, but the drink and the wild living became his downfall.

Christy was standing on my right, Davy to my left. With his flamboyant nature and Davy's strength how could I possible lose?

Billy Block Head came out like a bull, with his trousers hanging down, his backside in full view. The big Mayo man let a roar that would frighten Gulliver the giant. I ran around in circles laughing, avoiding all the wild swings that were coming in my direction, while the hardworking men cheered us on.

Their toothless expressions were divinely breathtaking. It was truly a sight to behold, with Johnny's nose and all those toothless smiles, it surely was a sculpture's paradise!

Along the old gable walls were six large arched windows, throwing in beams of light that shone down on us in heavenly glory. As Billy and I wrestled in floods of laughter, the dust from the old timber floor rose, creating a mass of smoke that looked like clouds. The wild birds flapped around us sending an echo-like sound around the room. I stood back and caught Billy with a few soft jabs. He gave up, reached for my hand, raising it in victory, his shirt bursting from the seams and sweat rolling from his brow.

When everyone left, Davy and I sat down on a timber barrel to eat our lunch.

"Georgie, you're like a butterfly that flew into my world," he blurted out. The cheese caught between his front teeth, created a perfect filling.

I was startled when he spoke those kind words and I wondered what book he had got them from.

"Here, George, have you got a girl?" he asked, jumping off the barrel.

He was still wearing his long coat, his towering voice filled with hope for his little friend. Then he shared with me, frame by frame, parts of his sad life. But he was overjoyed at the hope he saw in me as a young man.

"Remain all the days of your life a good man," he said smiling. Never drink, and Georgie, read books.

There's a girl out there for you George."

"George Fitzgerald? George Fitzgerald?" a man called.

I stood up. He walked towards us with a long piece of paper in his hand.

"Are you Fitzgerald?" he asked.

"That's me, the son of a king, or haven't yah read your history!" I replied jokingly.

"Son of a king or not, it's down the dole for you. We have to let yah go, work is short," he replied.

That Friday gates of the site were packed with men, some long haired, some toothless. I threw my bag across my shoulder and began shaking their hands. The rain was falling. I walked along the large timber fence when I heard someone call: "Here, Georgie, George."

I turned and saw that it was Davy. When he reached me, we just stared at each other for that awkward moment.

"You know the way I said that you were a butterfly. Well, you're an eagle and one day, you will fly with thousands of eagles behind you," he said.

I stood there in the rain, holding back the tears. He had ripped his coat while rushing to get to me - an encounter I had tried to sneak away from.

"Where will you be Davy?" I asked, biting my lip.

"I'll be standing on the largest mountain you ever did see. With my arm stretched out, waiting for the eagle to land."

We embraced. I left and walked away. I never did see Davy again, but a year later I received a letter from England. I couldn't understand the writing, but what I could make out was something to do with meeting Jesus and "I'll pray for you" - signed Davy.

♪

The year was 1982. It was a Saturday and the summer months had arrived. Music was bopping out from the door and windows of a nearby house. Men and women embraced the day with summer smiles, while heaps of children jumped up and down in front of the ice-cream van parked on the corner.

The summer project was on. This was set up by people in the area. Different outings and activities went on for about six weeks during summer. In the morning all the kids would gather in the schools for arts and crafts and much more fun things, to the delight of all the parents.

I saw Martina; she was standing on the corner dressed in a light blue dress. She had dark skin and a great singing voice.

"How're yah George? Are yah going down to the school?" she asked as I drew near.

"Yeah, come on, I'll walk down with yah," I replied swiping my arm into the air trying to catch a jinny-joe.

"I'm singing today," she said tipping my arm and then whispered, "Don't catch the jinny-joe, its bad luck."

"Don't be listening to that rubbish. Your voice will win them over; yah don't need luck."

She smiled, looked at me, and withdrew appearing greatly refreshed.

I was now entering the forest of adolescence. Not only were there physical changes taking place on the outside, but also changes in my heart. My attention was moving more and more in the areas of romance. It was creeping in through the music I listened to - Barry White and Marvin Gaye. I was about to cross the threshold that had a big sign pointing towards tomorrow. It said, "Only one way, no return." I wasn't aware of it then, but in that moment, my feet were carrying me along a road, to a place called Destiny.

The first thing we saw when we entered the gates of the school was a gang of kids. They were watching a man playing an accordion. He squeezed the box in and out and it spoke in a language that had its place in our past.

Older women danced, pulling up their long dresses so that their ankles were visible while the men tapped their feet and clapped their hands.

"I'll see yah later," Martina said as she rushed across the grass towards the stage.

"Yeah, best of luck with the singing," I shouted after her.

Toma, Joe and the boys were sitting at the wall, wrapped in the rays of the sun. Little Jack was standing beside them. He was a kid whose feet never stayed in one place for too long. He curtsied as if he was in the presence of royalty when I walked over, waving his hand in a dignified manner.

"Listen Jack me boy, the only prince yah need to see is the one that stares back at yah every morning."

He then drew himself up and grinned, evidently gratified with the compliment.

"Do yah think so, Georgie?"

"I know so," I replied as I bowed to him.

"Here, let Georgie sit down," he shouted, pushing the boys and throwing a few hasty glances on the off-chance that someone, anyone, heard what I had said. But nobody took too much notice of him.

A voice that crackled with excitement came to us from the corner. It whipped by us but we caught it.

"Yeah they're two brothers, I'm telling yah."

"The other brother, Natzi, is a great player so if we get them on our side we'll win, I'm telling yah."

"Here Pat, some blokes want yah to play ball with them," Joe said.

Pat went off smiling from ear to ear. But the thing they didn't tell him was the game was being played on the roof of the school.

To the passerby, it was just a flat roofed school-house in the middle of a working class neighbourhood. It acted as a place of education. But it was also a building, where on any given Sunday you would find the mass-goers, as the small red bricked building with the perspex windows acted as a church.

Since the birth of this neighbourhood back in 1973, there was never a church built, until much later on. In many ways, it was a landmark, in this great community of people. It was a football field, a music hall, a bingo hall, and a youth club. It was also a place where parents rested, in hopeful dreams for their children. At night it became a hub of activity. Boys with wild hair would stand on the corner drinking cider.

A few feet away there were a small number of steps that ran down to the yard. You could stare across the city, past the beautiful landscape of lush green fields and large trees.

On a clear night you could see the mountains. They stood with pride, like a giant watchdog, peering down into our world that was a cottage industry that boomed in human lives with both colourful and grim characters who were larger than life.

An old man would wink at us. His wink had a hidden meaning. It was one that only we knew. It said, "You're alright George - you're one of us."

It was a title I wore with pride because I loved my people and the neighbourhood I came from.

A few minutes into the game, Pat ended up in the toilet, but he was ok. We had such a laugh at that. "With him on our side we'll win."

"Yeah, win a quick exit to the jacks."

The smell of apples married in chocolate filled the air. It came from groups of makeshift stalls selling everything from candy floss to secondhand books.

We rolled the dice, played cards, laughing while chasing each other around the school.

The grounds fell into silence when Martina sang *Memories*. As the music reached a high pitch, I switch my glance. It was one of those 'over the shoulder' glances.

That's when I first saw her. She stood in the midst of a crowd of young girls. There she was, like a jewel in a crown, a flower blossoming on a beautiful spring day. Her dress was white, the whitest I'd ever seen. Her shoulder-length hair was dark brown. Her curvaceous body stood out among the crowd. I arched my back and tied my laces. Toma pulled deep on his cigarette and looked over at the girl in the white dress.

"What's the story, Toma?" I blurted.

"The story about what?" he asked as he stood up.

"About, that bird standing over there?"

"Oh yeah, that's Sandra, the one I told yah about."

I occupied my mind for a quick moment with a pleasurable stare, feeling like a man who had woken from a long sleep. My eyes were focused, taking everything in. I mustered up enough courage and began to walk across the crowded yard in my bare sunburnt skin, Bone's porcupine hat, and Paulo's sunglasses.

"What's happening Georgie?" a few boys shouted. I winked and disappeared into the crowd.

I heard a whisper, "Go over to her" one boy said to another. My ears were alert and my feet were now moving faster.

She stood very erect with a perfect posture. Her skin was dark brown and looked soft. But it was those beautiful blue eyes which didn't move or flinch that grabbed my attention.

"You have a lovely smile," I said, taking a deep breath.

"Thank you," she replied.

"You're one of the Fitzgerald's?" her friend said. "The boxer. You were in the paper a few weeks ago, me brother was telling us all about it."

A few weeks ago. That was months ago! I thought to myself, but said nothing.

I looked at her, caught her glare and fastened my lips as my heart skipped about ten beats. In the corner of my eye I caught a sight of a youth walking in our direction. He looked around her age or maybe a bit older. He was wearing his jeans in his boots. The collar on his shirt was turned up and his hands were deep in his pockets. She turned her head as if by design and smiled on his arrival. He stopped a few feet away and called her over.

"Listen, I've got to go," she said shyly.

I noticed she looked a bit embarrassed as she walked away. Her friends looked at me trying to see if my conscience was loaded down. I swallowed hard, but I remained straight-faced.

The school grounds were paved in eyes and in that moment, I felt they were all falling on me. We were standing in eyeshot of men with shirtless bodies, stacking boxes of sweets, toffee apples, and soft drinks. I pretended to be interested in them for a moment, hoping that while my eye was off her, she would be looking at me. After a few moments the boy walked away and her friends rushed over to where she was standing.

I watched her from a distance; she appeared free and in control, moving gracefully, like a beauty queen walking along a cat walk. She was confident, very much her own person. She was only fourteen-years old. She lived just a few feet away from the school, Billy Boy told me later.

A whirlwind had blown me into a world I did not know. At seventeen-years-of-age I was caught, smitten. I walked home that day with my brothers at my side. Joe had a crewcut and Pat's skin was so fresh and dark. Little Wesley was running in front. I walked like a sleepy child, like a man who was dropped, the blue canvas staring him in the face, but the man hadn't counted to ten yet.

On the way home we met Harry, a red-haired man who looked like a cross between James Cagney and Spencer Tracy. We had known Harry since we were young boys. He was the janitor of the neighbourhood. He would talk to us as growing boys, standing with his hands in his pockets lecturing us on the requirements for manhood.

"How do you catch a pearl?" I asked him.

He smiled, placed his hand on my shoulder and replied, "Pearls, they're among shark infested waters, yah should know that son."

"Yeah, I do know that Harry."

"To catch a pearl..." he paused for a long time looking up towards the afternoon sky, while taking a drag on his cigarette. "Become a pearl," he said with a giant smile, glaring at me. None of the boys had a clue what we were talking about but they all stared at him in their bare skin, T-shirts, caps, and sunglasses.

"Why a pearl?" I asked, deeply inquisitive.

"It's very simple, Georgie my boy, birds of a feather flock together."

When we began to walk away he called me back and placed his hands on my shoulders again. He spoke in a near whisper: "She's very beautiful."

"Who Harry?" I asked, pretending not to know what he was talking about.

"Your pearl in the white dress George," he said, with a grin.

"Yes Harry, her name is Sandra," I replied sheepishly.

"Become a pearl and you'll catch a pearl, right Georgie. Not just any old pearl Georgie, but a pearl of great choice."

That night I lay on the bed, and entered a make-believe world. My mind transported me to the very time, place, and moment I had first seen her. I closed my eyes and recalled her words; her eyes seemed to be imprinted in my mind.

I jumped up and opened the window. The air was fresh, the scent of summer filled me, its calmness was refreshing. I lay back down and imagined the world of love. Its complexities and its joys enhanced my spirit.

In my mind's eye, I walked across a large garden rich with orange trees and sweet smelling flowers. I slid in behind a warm breeze and took hold of a flower. Its petals were a wonderful blue, with veins of red running through it. The garden blossomed in the dazzling sun.

I wrote a message with the brush of my heart across the little petal:

"Like a cherry tree among cherry trees of the forest, your earrings dipped in gold, your body brown like the queen of Sheba in all her glory. So I watched you my dear. Let this little petal fly to you in the whistling of the night, as I close my eyes and drink deep of your scent, falling endlessly into the land of dreams."

ROUND 17

Toma emerged from behind his front gate and lit up a cigarette. It was a morning that appeared cheerful, but the wind was sharp in spite of the warm sun.

He shifted his eyes from left to right as he strolled down along the path. He appeared to be mumbling to himself, his mind caught up in a great complexity of thought. Then he lifted his head not so much towards the sky but in a more parallel position, so that he had a clear vision of anything that was in front of him.

He saw me just as I was about to turn the corner. He called to me and I watched him running. The soles of his shoes slid along the ground when he came to a sudden stop. He motioned with his hand for me to follow him. I did and we ran together, under the warm sun, towards the lane, a secret place, a place of story-telling.

We kept going through the maze of streets until we reached the end of the road and entered the lane. There we rested, breathing heavily with our hands on our knees. I was bent over, still breathing heavily, but in spite of this I threw a glance up the lane.

"Did yah hear the news about your man Slipper Boy?" he asked, speaking in between each breath.

"Na," I replied, a bit disappointed because I thought he was going to tell me something about Sandra. But I hid my disappointment.

"Why? What's the story?"

"The story is, he had a run-in with a hammer."

I concentrated on his face. His tongue was rolling off his mouth, and he was about to rush into the story when a kid called him.

"Here Toma, give us a go of your flick-knife."

"It's not a flick-knife, it's a camper knife."

He pulled it out of his back pocket, twirled it into the air, caught the handle, and buried it in the earth of a nearby garden.

The kid swiped it, and tried to copy him, but he looked clumsy. Toma swiped it back, shoving it into his back pocket.

"Now get up out of it, and leave us alone, or I'll give yah a clatter."

A clatter sounded good, but I left it to Toma to get rid of him. And he did.

"Wait till yah hear this," he said looking from side to side.

When he was finished telling me the story, I was shocked.

"Who told yah Toma?" I asked.

"Goatee, I met him up at the shops."

We were about to leave, when we saw Joe, Pat, and Weller coming towards us.

"Here George, you tell 'em, you have a way with stories," Toma said.

"Listen to this boys: did yah hear what happened to your man, Slipper Boy?"

"He's not my man," Weller said, when Joe cut in:

"Here you tell us Toma, he'll make a book out of it."

"Is that right, say nothing Toma. I'm telling it or no one's hearing it, right." So they all gathered around me as I recited the story.

"The lane was narrow, the muck that had seen generations pass was lodged on the side of the building, while the air sucked up

- 152 -

every foul smell that crept out of the nearby butchers, breathing it back into the lane, until every inch of the place was filled with the smell of a piggery.

"A boy stood back, afraid to move. Afraid to breathe, afraid because of what had happened...afraid for his life. He took another few slow steps back and nearly stumbled over a roll of old carpet. He glanced at the ground. His hand felt like it was frozen in a tight grip. It was only a short moment, but it seemed like a life time.

"His eyes were bulging, bloodshot, transfixed, and tense. He wished that someone would pluck them out; he wished; he wished that he hadn't come out that night. Then he looked at the hammer that was in his hand. Then he looked at the body. Pete the butcher boy dropped the hammer and cried, 'Yah should've left it Slipper Boy. Yah should have left it'. But he called a halt to his senses and covered the corpse with the carpet and ran."

"So Slipper Boy is dead?" asked the little kid who was hiding behind the wall.

No one commented.

Suddenly a shadow hovered over us; it was Father Wade. He ran the boxing at the school and knew Joe and I well.

"How'ya Father," we all said in unison.

"He's not my father," Noley our neighbour said after he just arrived.

"Have respect for the Father, Noley," Joe said sharply.

"Well boys, this is a bad day for the neighbourhood, a bad day," he said, bowing his head.

"It is Father," we replied together.

"But the Gardai will catch the blaggards, don't yah worry boys, and sweep this neighbourhood clean. Yah can be sure of that," he added.

"Yeah, they wanna have a good brush," Toma whispered.

"I thought I might see yis up at the school doing your boxing lads."

"Na Father, we gave it up. Joe has a girlfriend, her name is Jackie," I said, hoping that would take his mind away from boxing.

"Don't bring shame to your family, treat her nice," he said, tipping each of our caps and moving on.

We all walked out of the lane and spotted Git, Beanie and Ray standing on the corner so we headed up towards them. Paulie was coming down the other side of the street with Goatee by his side.

While we walked along the streets, I wondered if it really was Pete. I wondered if he would hand himself in. And I wondered if this would change him. That question would be answered, but not until we marched towards the new century.

By then he was all grown up, he was now an armed robber.

It's a blistering hot day. He jumps over a wall, into another lane landing on broken glass. He looks around him. He hears foot steps, coming towards him. So he runs, jumping over the roll of carpet. And as he is still in the air, he looks over his shoulder, and sees two men. One of them has a hand gun. It was the last thing he ever saw.

♪

The long black car crawled up along our streets; its mudguards had white rims on the outside that sparkled in the sunlight. Women stood in the shadows with their arms folded, while little children ran behind laughing and shouting

"It's a wedding car."

"Whose wedding, is it?" I asked, aware of all the laughing eyes, as Sandra stepped out of the car.

"Not yours anyway," a voice roared.

- 154 -

"Shut up," I said through the side of my mouth, not even bothering to look around.

"It's Mary's, yah know that girl? Sandra's mate. Well it's her older sister."

Again, I didn't even turn to see who commented.

"How is it going? I hope yah haven't forgotten about our date," I joked from across the street.

She gave me a gentle smile, but I read it carefully. It said, *who are you?*

The days passed but I couldn't get this girl Sandra out of my head. So I decided I would go and have a yap with Shay. On the way down I meet Papa the Bulldog. He was sitting on the little red brick wall. He had a full head of grey hair and he always carried a walking stick. Papa was a boxing fanatic.

"Papa, me head is done in over this bird."

"Don't let it," the grey-haired man said placing his hands on the top of the stick. His eyes were wide and attentive, his ears weren't slow to hear either. They were that low to the ground, I wondered how he managed to escape the passing cars. The rays from the sun brightened parts of his hair to nearly a perfect white that set off his Mafioso features.

"What will I do?" I asked.

"Georgie, wait until I tell yah. When I was about your age I worked the docks with me father. Anyway, we had this fella down there we called the Long Shore Man."

Papa stopped straight in the middle of a sentence, lifted his hand, and began to count. "There was me, the long fella, and little Sam. Now George, Sam had a sister, Maria. She was a bit too young for love, although every eye was on her, young or old. The Long Shore Man first saw her when he was standing at the stair of the tenements. His tongue could have cleaned the floor if he had the mind to. He tried everything he could to win her, but he nearly drove the father mad, and in the end he failed.

"What happened?" I asked with my own tongue cleaning the floor.

"Wait 'till I tell yah. The tide changed and things went well for Sam and his family. And in the course of time the Long Shore fella ended up working for them in their houses. He saw Maria everyday. But she had since married. See, he lived to see what he'd missed; he died in a dirty bed-sit a bitter man. Right son, here ends the lesson. I've got to meet Tony for a game of chess," he said rising to his feet

"Oh by the way Georgie, Maria told me years later, that he was the first man she'd ever really loved. All he had to do was wait. Georgie son, go and do likewise."

"Thanks Papa, catch yah later," I shouted as I jumped off the little wall and sprinted off towards my bike.

The sun was afar off and the wind blew behind me. I thought of Goatee's words: "May the wind blow you to your chosen destiny, brother?"

I went past the graveyard, said a prayer and moved on towards the old cobbler.

The sound of hammering could be heard as I approached the shop. I looked in and saw him bent over, chiselling away on a pair of shoes. What little sun there was shone through the small window, to the right of him.

"Well, well, the dead arose and appeared to many," he said with a chuckle, looking over the rim of his glasses.

He leaned over and put his arm around me.

"How is it going Shay?" I said, while pushing my bike in the door. I noticed he looked tired, or maybe he just looked older.

"Better for seeing you," he replied, with that famous smile.

In truth I was overjoyed seeing him myself. We greeted with a strong handshake.

After the old man recited a few jokes, he stuck on the burnt black kettle.

"We'll have a cup of coffee George. Sorry I don't have any biscuits, I'm slimming," he said, pointing to his mid- section.

He was delighted to hear that the boys were all doing fine. While he was talking, I gazed around the shop and wondered about the time that had gone by. It was like a leaf blowing in the wind. So it was here that I thought about yesterday.

My thoughts accompanied me to a little corner shop called Charity. Its brown timber doors were hinged on goodwill because this is what the old man who was dressed in the dark blue apron represented.

"Do yah remember when we were kids, Shay?" I asked glancing towards him.

My words granted him an invitation to bath in the summer time of his life. He bowed slightly and rested his hands on the window sill. I saw him stare through the old glass. He was looking for the little boys who played in his streets while on their way to the boxing club. There was a sparkle in his eye because he found them. That wonderful Santa Claus-smile made an appearance once again. That stare brought a strong sense of friendship that was fostered in an unbridled relationship, formed in the knowledge of a shared past.

He walked back to the counter, filled his mouth with small nails and hammered a pair of shoes.

"Remember George my boy; watch your own life with the eyes of a fox because when you become your own friend it will be hard to find an enemy. Plantations, plantations that's what life's about - plantations."

The man had a way with words. He was a master and a teacher in the game of life. His wisdom was deep and hidden.

"I see what you're saying, but I don't understand," I replied.

"Ah," he said with a great burst of joy. "You've bitten the bait, so now you're ready to understand."

"Life is like a great plantation that is worked on everyday. You first must sow and then wait for the weeds to grow. As you pull up the weeds you will see the bird of the air flying over to snatch the seed. That's when you need to watch your life because when the bird sees you watching. He stays far away."

"I know what yah mean, Shay," I said, not really sure if I did. "I have a bit of a problem."

"Women trouble, eh?"

"Yeah. I guess you could say that."

I began to roll the story off my lips at a hundred miles an hour.

"Slow down, slow down," Shay cut in. "George my boy, as you know, I never married. But what I will say is that if you get close enough, she'll see your heart."

Sitting on the chair, listening to Shay, I began to feel encouraged. And as he spoke to me, a thought crossed my mind: *Here was this old man - alone. Did he miss out? Did he lose the girl of his dreams?*

My heart was filled with compassion for my old friend when I thought about him walking through life alone.

"Georgie, one man finds a wife, the other finds something else. Maybe it's work, sport or books. But both share the same happiness in life."

The old fox had seen my heart and gently relieved me of any burden.

"Will you ever give up the shop, Shay?" I asked, diverting from my life for a moment.

"I will,' he said, the famous smile making an appearance again. "See that wall over there George" he said, pointing to the large grey stone wall, the house of the dead.

"This place will go, when they take me over the wall to my place of rest," he said laughing.

Toma and the boys were standing on the corner when I reached our street.

The clouds gathered and a sharp wind howled unexpectedly just as the rain fell. A woman placed empty milk bottles at the step while schoolboys ran with pockets full of marbles trying to knock them down. One of them ran into me, and then raced off.

"Here!" I shouted, and when I turned, I saw Sandra and her boyfriend standing across the street. He kissed her and walked away. A sudden downpour of rain pelted the streets. She began to run. Everyone rushed indoors and fathers and mothers called their kids from the street.

I stood, and watched her disappearing and then I ran.

"What's the story George?" Joe called as he stood under the wall capping.

I turned for a moment, looked back at Weller, Toma, Noley, Paulo and the rest, standing in the rain. We stared at each other for a moment. I took my hat off, and bowed. Toma walked out in front, wearing the same cap as me, he shouted;

"Run George run, and don't look back."

And that's what I did.

I raced under the pouring rain, across the streets, down the lane, past the gang drinking cider and the women rushing for the bingo. A stolen car skidded; I rolled over the bonnet and kept going with Shay's words rushing through my mind, "If yah get close she'll see your heart."

She turned the corner, and stopped for a moment. Her hair was flat from the rain, her clothes tight, lining her body. The thunder loomed in the night sky, roaring like a man of war.

Staring at me through her deep blue eyes, she rolled her wet hair into one simple braid. I felt a rush go through me like a symphony as I held back each blink that tried to interrupt the moment.

Instrumental music was coming from a nearby window. Men and boys looked back as they jumped out of the car. I saw Bop and Maria running past with umbrellas, they saw her and called out. But we were pinned together by a glance that floated across the street, dodging between the heavy drops of rain.

She lifted her head and raised her eyes. It was a seductive look. She smiled, and let the wind carry her away, until all that was left was a memory.

ROUND 18

The following days and weeks vanished as if they'd never appeared at all. Everything was a haze, a daydream, a fantasy. I began to spend more time alone. In the evening I would sit in the backgarden, where I would sketch love hearts putting her name inside. Then I'd scribble it out not to leave any evidence. It felt safe and comfortable, sitting under an umbrella of my daydream world.

A tenderness I had not known appeared. I welcomed it, but then I hid it like a man burying treasure.

"The pen is mightier than the sword," I heard ma say many times. So I decided to write a letter. I pulled a pen from the drawer. Placed the white paper on the table, stared at it, lifted the sheet, blew over it and scanned it again. Then the pen began to talk.

My heart that had been locked up for so long felt a liberating power rush through as the words appeared. It was the character that inspired me and for a tiny moment, a moment that smiled at me. I wasn't afraid and I didn't feel like a stupid boy.

In the orchard of dreams, in the world of men, there is one that is the finest specimen that was given to us as a gift, in the garden of perfection - a woman!

When I finished, I sealed it, without signing it. Hours passed, the night slept and morning appeared. It was a Sunday and I knew the paper boy would be delivering his papers. So I jumped on my bike and cycled through the streets.

Once I reached the block, I waited. And sure enough like clockwork there he was.

"Do they get a paper in that house?" I asked

"Yep."

"Will yah do me a favour?" I said, handing him two pounds.

"Yep. What is it?"

"Will yah give that to the bird that lives in there, if she opens the door? Don't give it to anyone else."

"No problem, Twinny," he said looking at me with smiling eyes.

I waited for a few moments. He came out gave me a wave and moved next door. That night the streets were deserted. I sat on the wall and watched out for her. She usually came home around this time I thought.

Although it was still early, darkness was beginning to creep in. I caught a glimpse of a young girl rushing towards the lane. I knew it was Sandra. Without a pause or a moment's thought when consideration would counsel me, I jumped off the wall and moved across the street.

I reached the end of the lane. I heard rough voices. She appeared startled, rushing down the street, while throwing a glance over her shoulder every now and again. So I crossed the grass, careful not to add to the fright she seemingly received. She stopped and looked behind her.

As the daylight dimmed, the clouds gathered, and the wind joined in. It was the only voice that could be heard as we stood there in silence.

"Are yah alright?"

"Yeah, I'm fine," she said with a slight quiver. "There was a gang in the lane and I just got a fright, that's all."

"Listen, I'll be standing at the wall every night, so if yah want, I'll walk down with yah."

She opened her eyes wide. I swallowed hard.

"Can I ask you a favour then?"

"Yeah what is it?"

"If you walk home with me, let it be at a distance. That's all it will be. I have a boyfriend."

"Yeah, that's all right." I never really imagined that she would be my girlfriend anyway. I knew I was living in hope.

"Can I walk with yah now?"

She hesitated, but smiled and said, "Yes."

"Who are yah looking at," cried a loud voice.

I stepped away from Sandra. Charlie, one of Johnny B Goods mates stepped out of the lane. He moved towards me with two shuffling steps and threw a boot into the air. He was dressed in Dexy's Midnight Runners' dungarees. He violently bumped off me.

"Is there something wrong?" he screamed, throwing his arms into the air.

"Not at the moment," I muttered.

I felt his gaze rest on my neck as I walked away. I tipped Sandra's shoulder and whispered, "Come on, let's get out of here."

"Here are yah a chicken or what, Twinny? Twinny, the big man from the South, the boxer, a chicken."

Da's words rang in my ear, "George, Joseph, I knew boys like that in Ballyfermot and nothing good ever came of them, walk away son."

I looked over my shoulder and tipped my hat back. He smeared the cider from his mouth and stared at me wildly.

"Is that boy calling you again?" she asked faintly.

I could tell by her voice that she was hoping he wasn't. I paused for a moment. She squeezed my hand. It was then I noticed that I was holding it.

"Is that your bird, Twin?"

I said nothing, wondering if he was the one that cut Sonny.

"Are yah deaf?" he blasted.

"Let's get out of here," I stuttered as I turned away, still holding her hand.

"Will he come after us?" she asked nervously.

"Na, don't be worrying. Here, is there something in me eye?" I asked, as I turned towards her.

She looked closely. I looked closer, and noticed he was gone.

"No, I can't see anything, it's too dark," she replied.

"Yeah neither can I. It was only a fly, only a fly."

"George, were you afraid?"

"Na, I got things in me eye before."

She stopped, withdrew her hand and burst out laughing.

"You've some sense of humour," she said, between each breath.

"I am a man full of surprises," I replied.

It was only a ten minute walk to her house but I tried to walk as slow as I could. All the nervous small talk disappeared and we began to enjoy the first few moments of a calm conversation.

I looked across the road and noticed Timothy Anderson. He was walking in quick steps. Then he relaxed his pace, turned his face into a window of a car and smiled. He wet the tips of his fingers, pushed back his eyebrows and turned his head.

"Oh yah look lovely, Sandra," he beamed as he approached us.

Timothy Anderson was a boy who had his head stuck in a book. Or at least, that's how I remembered him. But now he looked mature, fresh-faced, full head of golden hair, fine physique and a narrow waist.

To the right of him, two youths crossed the street, dressed in caps and polo necks.

"Here Twinny," they called.

Timothy was moving closer. I stepped back and bid the boys to move on, with a quick motion of my hand. They got the message, winked and moved on.

"How's your studying coming along? Are yah reading that book I told yah about?" he asked Sandra.

Before she could answer, he lurched towards her, his arm clutching her forearm and he stood smiling like the Cheshire cat. I stood there, arms at my side, not knowing what to do, completely surprised by his forwardness.

"No, but I think it's on the curriculum for next year," she replied.

"Well, I would suggest you read it. Do yah have a copy?"

"No."

He stood back, placed his hand on his chin and muttered to himself.

"Do you know what? I just happen to have a copy at home. I'll drop it down to you," he quickly added.

"Look, there's no need," she replied shyly. "Oh by the way, this is my friend George."

"Yes, yes, the boxer fella. Now listen, I'll come down and help you with the book, if yah need help."

"I bet yah will," I thought, looking at him sharply.

He turned quickly, and asked, "Do yah want me to walk down with yah? I'm going down to a mate, not far from where you live. I'll walk yah home Sandra."

I felt a stabbing pain. She looked from him to me and back again.

"I'd better get going. Sure the boys are probably looking for me anyway," I said lowering my eyes to avoid meeting theirs.

I walked away with my hands in my pocket and my cap pulled down. I turned back and saw her brother Robert, and his girl-friend Grainne standing on the street waiting on her. She quickly said something to Anderson, left him there and raced across the street, her fishtail skirt swaying in the breeze. Then she turned and waved at me.

♪

Sonny had survived the assault. The blade that struck him missed his jugular. But it did catch him on the side of the face, leaving a lasting memory of a thick reddish scar, which no amount of soap could wash away.

The boy that cut Sonny will wake up in a dormitory in the middle of the night and see another inmate searching his belongings. He will leap out of his bed, pull a scissors from under his pillow and stab the boy to death. Sonny was blessed to be alive.

♪

It was a Friday night. Joe, Pat, and I were in town playing pool. Joe glanced up at the clock.

"Where's Sonny? I thought he was going to meet us here?" he asked Pat, who in turn asked me the same question.

"He said he'd be here, maybe he got detained," I replied. The night passed quickly and it was getting late, well it was eight o' clock. Ma wanted Pat home for nine. So we placed the cues on the table and left. When we got home our uncle Packy was there sitting at the fire talking to our da about politics.

"What's the story Packy?" I said as I walked in the door.

"Which one do yah want to hear, the one about the three bears?" he replied laughing.

Packy had been a boxer, he wore the broken nose to prove it, but he had brains to burn. That's what ma said. He loved to talk about books, so did ma. Da read a book a week.

I sat and listened to them talk about books on the Famine, then they turned their conversation to Joyce and a book called the Dubliners. Packy said it was the best piece of English ever written. They then talked about Behan and *The Borstal Boy*; I loved to listen to all the stories. Packy said the old English language was wonderful and full of colour. He had read the *King James Bible* and had just finished a book by Dante.

"Dickens was a genius," ma said.

"That's because he had mastered shorthand," da said, adding: "He wrote 'Oliver' when he was twenty-two-years-of-age."

Packy jokingly recited some of Dickens' work in an old English accent. We all laughed, I thought it was great.

Sonny had given me a bible when he got out jail. He said God was talking to him. I thought he was off his head. But I went upstairs and pulled it out from under the bed. I liked the big one da had because that had pictures, I loved the pictures. The one Sonny gave me was old and it had no pictures. But I opened it anyway and read, *'Confess with your mouth, the Lord Jesus and believe in your heart that God raised him from the dead and you'll be saved.'* I liked that word so I walked around the room like Packy speaking it out. But it didn't sound great in a Dublin accent so I spoke in old English one, but that didn't sound great either, so I switched it to an American accent like John Wayne and that sounded great. I sat on the bed wondering if God talked like John Wayne.

I heard Packy leave and then da called me from downstairs. When I reached the bottom step he nodded for me to follow him into the sittingroom. Ma averted my gaze, something was up I thought.

"Right George, I won't waste time, I'll get straight to the point." I was on the bus last night and that Goatee fella was in front of me. Yah want to hear the talk out of him. So the bottom line is, I don't want you or Joseph to be with him. Is Joseph out?"

"Ehh, yeah, I think so. But, Da."

"Don't but da me, that's it."

"He's alright Da. He's alright. We'll he's ok."

He shrugged his shoulders and said, "Listen, I met boys like that in Bally'er, nothing good ever came of them. Walk on son." Yah mean."

"I mean it now. That's it. I'll have a word with the Joseph fella when he gets in."

I walked back up the stairs. I wanted to give Goatee a box over his big mouth. And then I wondered how I was going to tell him.

See that's the thing, the streets bully you, trying to force you to abandon all the moral rules that you were brought up to believe in. If you don't join in you're a coward. Its voice is very powerful. It can sneak up on you, rip your heart out and before you know it you're lying on the ground staring up at the policeman asking, "What happened how did I get here?"

I was standing in the valley of decision. I wondered how Goatee didn't see my da behind him. Then I thought: He did see him. "If Goatee comes up tomorrow with back-up he knows I'm angry," I heard myself say.

The next morning Goatee walked up the street as if he was a lord with his head in the air and his shoulders held back. He had three other boys with him, they were dressed in raggy clothes.

"Hear yah missed it last night. We robbed a gaff. Anto got shot, but he's ok." Sonny and him got locked up, I got away," he said smiling.

"Shut your big mouth," I roared.

"What did yah say?"

His friends stood back with their fists clenched. Toma and Joe did the same thing.

"Goatee yah heard me, right and you're not going to do anything about it, right." Everything went quiet but Goatee broke the silence by telling us the story anyway.

"We parked the car in a field about a half a mile away from the gaff. And then we crawled along the field towards the gaff."

"Don't make such noise," Sonny shouted in a whisper to Anto as three pairs of mucky shoes crossed the back garden.

"I'm not a thick, yah know what I mean Sonny" Anto replied, speaking through his nose.

Sonny muttered a few curses when his foot went down into a black hole but we kept creeping until they reached the back door.

"Yah know where a lot of these blokes keep their money," Sonny said, as we stood at either side of the door.

"In the bank," I said.

"Yeah right Goatee that's why we're here, up to our necks in muck. They keep it under their pillows."

"Man I never thought of that one. It's a good place to hide money, no one would be wide, yah know what I mean," Anto then said.

"Ah forget it."

There was a small window with criss-crosses in the glass and rusty bars on the outside, but the back door was free from any shutters.

"Here hold onto that jammybar, I can't pop these doors without it."

Taking hold of the handles he began to pull them towards himself at the same pace and rhythm. And in only a few moments the doors popped open like a cork on a champagne bottle. So in we walked.

The three boys with Goatee stood staring at us and I was growing more angry as I listened to his story.

"Here Goatee you're a mouth, Noley our neighbour shouted."

He is a mouth, I thought to myself as Noley walked on. But Goatee was not put off, he just kept going.

There was an old couch, two chairs, and the fire was still smouldering. We moved around the kitchen at incredible speed, emptying drawers, turning over chairs, and pulling up rugs. But we found nothing.

Sonny pointed to the stairs. Anto went first. I went second and Sonny followed. But before he did, he opened the hall door and jammed it with a piece of paper, just on the off chance we had to leave in a hurry.

The landing was large in a diamond shape that had four doors set around it. The floorboards were loose and noisy, but us gentlemen were adapted to such problems. Goatee said laughing.

"Do yah know what we did?"

"What? Tell us Goatee," the boys said.

But I cut in by shouting, "Just get on with it will yah."

"We rested our right feet on the large skirting board, while our left feet remained on the floor. And by springing into the air a little, allowing the pressure to fall down on our feet, we crossed it with ease, not a single sound.

The first thing that hit us when we entered the bedroom was a repulsive smell. Sonny pulled up his jumper and covered his nose, while Anto followed suit. But I stood at the door and slowly moved to the end of the bed. Sonny took one side.

The heavyset farmer was snoring loudly, lying on the bed in his clothes. His head was divorced of hair, except for the backs and sides.

"I bet, Sonny thought he was Jack, robbing the giant, in Jack and the Beanstalk," Toma laughed.

"Sonny's no Jack and he's no Robin Hood," Noley said, walking by again.

"Shut your mouth and go home and get your books out, Goatee snapped.

"At least I have a brain, something you don't have," Noley, replied.

"Here will yah let him finish the story," Joe said sharply.

"Sonny pushed his hand under the pillow and felt the wad of notes, but the farmer was lying on it. It was concealed in the lining of the pillow. He pressed up the button on the Stanley blade, cut through, and reached his hand in. He glanced over at Anto who was still holding his breath.

He had good reason to because right underneath him was an old pair of boots that were the size of canal boats. Your man stirred and turned his head. Sonny moved his hand deeper. The farmer moved again. Sonny rolled the money and pulled it out. As we were about to leave, Sonny spotted a bulge in the man's shirt pocket but his arms were folded, leaning across the top. So he bent down and ran the blade across the bottom and pressed two of his fingers up ever so gently rolling the largest bunch of fifty pound notes I'd ever seen.

Anto couldn't hold on any longer. He needed air. When he reached the door he released his breath and inhaled every foul smell that his lungs could hold. His face went white and he vomited all over the floor.

The farmer jumped up with a face on him that looked like he possessed an evil sprit. We ran for the door descended the stairs in great speed with the man chasing after us hot on our heels.

Running further and further into the darkness, with the sense of this mad oul fella following us sent our hair standing on our necks. The boys turned their faces towards the house. That's when we saw what looked like a shotgun in his hand. A sound like a thousand voices rang in the air and Anto fell.

"I'm shot Sonny, I am shot," Anto cried. Sonny and me grabbed his arm.

"Come on keep going."

He staggered to his feet and escaped through a maze of trees and bushes. Then we slid into a river. Anto was filled with terror, trembling cold sweats pouring out of him, while the blood ran down his arm. We could hear footsteps, crunching on fallen branches and heavy breathing as the farmer charged past. We waited there 'till there was no longer a sign of the man.

"Come on," Sonny said, as we moved up river crawling out a few feet away from the car. Sonny dragged Anto under a tree and ripped through his coat with a Stanley blade.

"Its only pellets... its only pellets," he said, before running for the car.

"Get in Anto," Sonny shouted.

The sound of the car starting alarmed the farmer. The farmer was running. The wheels were spinning. The engine was roaring.

"Duck!" Anto shouted.

Sonny kept one hand on the steering wheel, and one hand, on the accelerator. As we drove off at great speed, the front window went in and the car spun out of control, hitting a tree. Next thing we saw was the blue flashing lights of the patrol cars. I rolled out of the car and hid behind the bushes but the boys were arrested.

The police were bringing them to the nearest garda station, when I overheard a radio call come in, informing them about a stabbing that had occurred in Finglas. A youth was dead. The officer asked the radio controller if the youth had been identified.

"Not yet, but we have a lead, a few local kids told us that he went by the name Johnny B Good."

"Yeah old news Goatee, we heard it on the news," I said.

I had my back to the wall, we were facing each other, no one said anything. I felt pity for him then, what else did he know. But it was my chance to do what da said. Goatee's mates stared at us with their fists clenched.

"Here, them pair killed more people than heart attacks," Joe said laughing, pointing to Goatee's mates.

"Yeah the Westside Boys, us Southies aren't good enough," I then added.

We laughed but the boys looked even angrier. So after Goatee gave out a few harsh words he walked off with his three little pals. I knew now I had to watch my back, but that's just the way it was.

The next morning, I hung over the front gate listening to the vegetable man hollering. I'd heard the news on the radio again. It gave out Johnny B Good's real name, and his age, he was nineteen-years-old.

As I stood day-dreaming I noticed a young girl heading in my direction.

"Now that's a pretty sight," the vegetable man beamed as he passed, while his boys ran into the gardens placing cartons of eggs on the front steps.

I was wearing a white grandfather shirt, blue-jeans, and a grey porcupine hat. I tipped it back and adjusted my vision, taking a deep breath because I recognized the girl. It was Sandra. My heart skipped a beat as I was filled once again with a familiar sense of joy.

"Hi, how's it going?" she said softly.

Her hair was tied back in a tight bow; she wore long earrings and a short dress. In the few short weeks I hadn't seen her, she had really matured. I mentioned it jokingly. She blushed, turned her head, and smiled.

The sound of the street awaking settled us both, as we basked in the warm sun. There were too many hidden faces hanging around, so I broke the silence with a suggestion.

"Do yah want to go for a walk?"

"Well I'm just going to the shop, then I'll walk with yah," she said sheepishly."

So off we went and walking side by side past the cluster of houses along the narrow road until it emptied itself of the working class houses.

I had my hands behind my back, trying desperately to think of something to say. We walked for some time until we reached the grounds of the local hospital. To the right was a beautiful garden with a timber fence. Sandra was a bit reluctant but I persuaded her to come in and rest. I sat on a cushion of tiny yellow flowers while she sat across from me with her back against a tree. She leaned over, took my hat and placed it on her head.

"What was it like to be a boxer?" she asked, balancing my hat on her head. "Well, there's boxing gloves and a ring," I replied laughing.

"You know that's not what I meant," she said, slightly thumping my arm.

"Alright then, there's a canvas that pulls on your legs, the rope burns the back of your neck and you feel the most horrible fear imaginable. And the cold, that's not great either."

Her eyes screwed up. "If you're so afraid, why did you box?"

"Courage is fear strangled. Everyone feels it, it's part of the game.

Anyway, forget that."

"Are you any good in school? I asked, placing a little flower behind her ear.

"I am not really sure. I got honours in the mocks," she replied.

"I knew who you were, the day you approached me in the schoolyard. Everyone knows – Twinnys, the boxers," she said.

"Yeah I knew you as well." What I meant was, I'd heard of her, but I didn't tell her that.

"But see your school-work, keep going at it."

"Were you good in school?" she asked.

"Yeah, I was so special they put me in a special row and gave me a special name."

I saw a ladybird so I picked it up and placed it on a leaf.

"It's very pretty" she said.

When I turned towards her I noticed a great look of surprise on her face.

"Ah look at his eyes, they appear so sorrowful," she said moving closer.

"Do you know what I think of a lot?"

"What's that?" she asked.

"I think about the stars."

"The stars," she said, looking at me even more strangely.

"I often wonder how many stars there are. Where the snow goes in summer? And why animals have no reason? And the sea, where it starts and how does it know where to stop?"

"So you're a deep thinker. I suppose that's pretty special."

She walked over towards a brown fence to where a horse was. She removed the bow, allowing her hair to fall freely. I stood up and asked her nervously if she would like to dance.

"Yah like to dance?" she said, creasing her forehead trying desperately not to laugh.

"Yeah...but only in the company of another dancer."

She blinked at me and turned away. There was moment of silence.

The light wind blew across her hair. She turned quickly towards me, brushing her hair off her face. It was a perfect movement, a combination of bright eyes and the calm of the day that claimed my heart.

"What happened with your boyfriend?" I asked as we walked home.

"I am meeting him tonight," she said, breaking the silence. I decided not to push her on the boyfriend thing. When we reached the school we met her friends. They stood together talking and laughing.

"Someone was looking for yah earlier, Sandra," Bop said. Then I heard her say, "Who?"

"Some blonde fella, Tim. Timothy Anderson. He was talking to us for ages, I think I'm in love," Bop beamed.

I waved and walked away. Then I remembered I was going to see Sonny later.

Mr and Mrs Thomson were in their garden, pulling up the weeds. They were a couple that were stuck together, if one went in the other followed, if one came out the other wasn't far behind.

"There yah are George, or is it Joe?" Mr. Thomson asked.

"How's it going? Are yah hard at it?" I replied trying to move on.

"Off out somewhere nice?" he then asked.

I wasn't getting away that easy.

"Yeah, I'm just going to visit my friend."

"Ah that's good of yah. Is he sick or something?" he said, moving closer to the wall

"Well that's one way of putting it."

"When's he getting out?"

"Looka! There's me bus, I'll see yah later," I shouted, dashing across the road, nearly tripping over a couple of kids playing in the streets.

I jumped off the bus at Harts Corner. The rain was beginning to fall heavily, but despite this, I walked with a sense of joy because I was looking forward to seeing Sonny, although the joy rolled up into a ball and vanished into mid-air as the timber door closed behind me.

♪

Have you ever been in a place you really felt you shouldn't be? Or maybe dreamed of a place, saw it in your mind, painted it with the brush of your heart. But in reality it was nothing like you had imagined? Well, when I crossed through the door of St Patrick's, I stepped into a world massively more repulsive than I had ever dreamed of.

Webbed together in a penal system that dated back to the Victorian times were boys who lived together. Their lives were cemented like the grey joints that ran along the black stone walls. They were dressed in grey trousers and green type shirts. Their hair was cut short and they had long drawn faces. The tallest of them, wore trousers too short and you could see their ankles.

An army of blue suits filled the outer area and the air itself seemed to be dipped in despair. I was a visitor, a free man, among the chained hard faced boys.

The guards wore dark blue suits with lines of silver buttons. Chains and keys rattled, sending a chilling echo, like a voice that cried in the darkness. Redemption was a word used in a different galaxy for many of these troubled boys.

A large guard, with the face that had itself been in prison too long, handed me a small piece of paper with Sonny's name on it. I was then shown a small room that housed the visitors.

In the corner of the room, a woman sat with a child. She wore a scarf, with strands of grey hair making an appearance, just above her forehead. Her clothes were unkempt and her face bore no wrinkles. It was a young face that had traveled too many roads, too hard, too early. Her thin body seemed to be lost in her dark coat. She sat beside an old man, who coughed so much, I thought he might fall over and die.

The stocky man with long-hair whose face seemed to be made out of cast iron, lit up a cigarette and stared at me. I stood in silence glaring over at my cast-iron friend, who contributed very little as far as comfort was concerned. So I walked out the door feeling a bit sick.

It was a grey windy day and the sound of the heavy door crashing shook me.

"What's the story Twinny?" a voice called, startling me even more. It was Nicky.

"I'm here to see Sonny, Nicky."

"Na yah won't be able to see him. They took him down the base," he replied with a sour smile.

We stood and talked for a moment or two, until he was dragged off by a guard. I walked back to the room and when I did, I thought I saw Goatee, running across the yard with two guards running alongside him.

I thought about Nicky and the Story he once told me, the story of his life.

He was born in the heart of the city on a cold November morning. The women of the tenement rushed out of the room with basins of water and cloths that were soaked with blood. Nicky's ma died on that cold morning, in the inner city of Dublin. His sisters and brother, the one they call Mousey, waved goodbye to him as he was shipped off to relatives who lived on the north-side.

Their father liked the pub and eight mouths to feed became too much for him. An uncle who had a glass eye, and a smileless face reared Nicky and his brother. But every Christmas, Mrs Murphy a neighbour from the inner city would arrive with sweets for the boys. And when alone she would recite the story of their birth saying, "remember boys your ma loved yah."

A guard called Sonny's name. I stood up. He handed me the small paper with his name on it and it informed me that Sonny was in Mountjoy.

"Thanks," I said and headed towards the small door that was set among the big door.

"Follow me," shouted a tall guard as I passed.

The guard shrugged his shoulders and again shouted, "Follow me."

I side-stepped him as two boys walked on handcuffed. I looked over my shoulders, startled by the appearance of the boys. It was Peter and little John my boyhood friends in Ballymun.

Peter stopped and stared at me, the rain was falling. I could see him searching my very soul. John smiled, it was haunting.

"Come on boys," the guard shouted.

"All right George," Peter said forcefully.

"All right Peter, all right John," I muttered back as I headed towards one door and they headed towards another.

One day I would go back to Ballymun only to find that both boys were dead.

While walking towards the bus stop, my spirit was silent. I felt a great emptiness inside. I hoped for light, one flame of light that had the power to expel the darkness.

ROUND 19

Suddenly she was gone. Her presence had vanished. She had finished with her boyfriend. That was the news that filtered through the grapevine.

Night after night I would go over in my mind the great conversations we had. Like a detective, seeking out any clues, as to whether or not she had any feelings for me. Her disappearance confirmed what everyone was thinking. No one gave me a chance, but that was nothing new, they never did.

Finally I came to the conclusion that I was only fooling myself. A thought had crossed my mind to call to her home. But that thought was invaded by the stark reality that she was only fourteen years and I was eighteen years.

She was in bed at 9.30.

I was only going out at 9.30.

She went to school.

I went to work.

She watched children's programmes.

I watched adult programmes.

She drank coke.

I drank beer.

She stood on one mountain. I stood on another, with a massive gulf between.

I had stepped into a valley of raging winds. The haunting familiar sounds of a lonely dark corner exhausted me. I had asked a few boys if they had seen Sandra. They said that she was going out with some new bloke now.

When I arrived home I went up to my bedroom. The door opened and in walked my ma.

"Are you alright George?" she asked in a soft voice.

"Yeah Ma, I'm grand."

"Are yah, sure?"

"Yeah, I swear I'm ok."

"It's just, your father's worried about you."

"There's nothing to worry about."

"Do you want something to eat?"

"No thanks Ma." We always said thanks. Ma said it was a sign of a good person.

Out on the streets I was Twinny, tough, maybe even hard. But inside in the bedroom, I was just George.

"Maybe you need to go out and see a film?" she said.

They never encouraged drinking.

"Na I'm ok, I'm just a bit tired from working."

Wesley brought me a cup of tea, the little mite. He was only six years old then.

"Thanks, Wes."

"I ate your chocolate da sent up."

"That's ok," I smiled back.

"Listen, If you want to talk we'll be downstairs."

"Ok Ma."

Pat came in after ma had gone and handed me a new album. Now Pat never gave out his records. It was Prince, I think.

"Thanks Pat."

"No problem," he said, walking out, leaving the door open.

A few minutes later I heard the hall door open. Da was downstairs talking to Joe. He came up.

"Here George, do you want to go for a pint?"

"Na," I said.

"What's the story?" he looked concerned. His face was red from the night air.

"Nothing, everyone is doing my head in. Just leave me alone."

"Da said there's a good film on downstairs."

"What's the name of it?"

"Ben Hur."

So I left my solitary confinement and entered the sittingroom. The fire was blazing and the sound of the logs crackling in the fire brought me great comfort. Da looked over at me. He smiled and rubbed his hands together.

"This is a brilliant film, you'll love it."

He was right, I did.

After the film, I felt refreshed and I began to doubt the rumours I had heard earlier about Sandra. So I went out and met Bop, Sandra's best friend.

"Where is Sandra?"

Bop paused for a moment, placing her hand behind her head. Bop then looked at me.

"She's not allowed out, that's why I am up here. I was looking for you, to tell you that you can't see her anymore. Her ma found out that she was seeing a man of twenty years."

I could see in her eyes that she didn't like relaying this message. But I still protested.

"I'm not twenty! Who told them that? Anyway what do yah mean I'm seeing her? I am only seeing her, the way I see you and the rest of the girls. We're just friends that's all, you know that."

"Well that's all I can say, best leave things the way they are."

I turned and moved quickly up the street not looking behind. I ran as fast as I could. The winter night air was sharp, cutting across my face. I walked into the house.

Ma and da were still watching the TV with a big fire still blazing. I held a tight face, took my coat off, and hung it over the chair.

"Do yah want a cup of tea?" ma asked.

"It's ok, I'll make it myself," I replied, keeping my face to the wall.

The little boy inside was comforted by the parental voice. I wanted to rush and tell her, but the young man reasoned, so I kept my face to the wall, placing the kettle on the element listening to its hissing sound.

I poured a cup of coffee and went into the sittingroom. I walked back into the kitchen and then back into the sitting room. Blinded by tears, I ran into the bedroom and closed the door. I put on Michael Jackson and sat on the bed. I stood up again and walked around the room talking myself into a state of panic, calling myself names. I felt my soul had betrayed me.

I believed I was strong, placing watchmen on the doors of my heart and yet I had fallen like a man in war. My act of admission was deepening the wound. I was blinking my way through this nightmare. I grabbed the bed and squeezed hard. Over the last few months there was only one photograph in my mind, it wasn't even developed, but now it was ripped in two.

The music from the stereo tugged at my emotions, as I once again gazed out of the window. I thought of those bright blue enquiring eyes that were full of innocence, her perfect manner and the curvy body, awaiting the arrival of a college boy. The thought cut me deep, stabbing into my heart.

For the first time, I was seeing a side of me that the mirror didn't reveal. Was I panicking? No - I was manic. I began to shadow box as if I could fight this with my fists. I didn't stop until my body was dripping in sweat. I sat back down, my body, soul and mind spent. Ma's famous words sprang to mind: "First you don't succeed, try, and try again."

The light went on in my mind so I sat down and wrote Sandra's mother a letter. Then I ripped it up and started again. All I wanted to do was walk down the street with Sandra holding her hand and say, "Here look! I have a girlfriend."

I stood in the corner like the boy I once knew, my hands pressed hard against my face. Reason crept in and it filled my mind. Its sting was deadly. "You have fooled yourself my little friend, look at you now curled up in a corner. What would a beautiful fourteen-year-old want with an eighteen-year-old-ex -prize-fighter!"

I lay back down on the bed and slowly drifted to sleep.

I awoke in the early hours. The window was left open, a light breeze blew in. It sent a chill across my body.

I stared up at the ceiling for a long time, while I placed a hard mask on, one I could hide behind. Pain is no respecter of people, rich man, poor man, beggar man, thief, it doesn't matter, it comes to us all. I looked towards the window.

The morning sky was bright. A hushed silence fell on our streets. It was here I saw, through my mind's eye the most dramatic scene. My hand reached across the rooftops. It was chained in the darkness of an eclipsed sun, but another hand reached out for mine as the slave ships of separated time passed by. It was soft and gentle with a deep wound in the centre. We touched each other and there I cried.

"No more time wasted and no more veils of separation." The four winds were held back. I looked up and saw, beams of light coming from the early morning sun.

Time drifted by, slowly as the long days turned into weeks. One Sunday morning, I lay in bed with cemented eyelashes, they flickered and then opened. The light that splintered through the dark clouds ran across the carpet on the floor. My first thought was Sandra. A few weeks had dragged past since I'd seen her. Toma and I had gone on the beer the night before and fell home.

I was quick about getting dressed before ma caught a hold of me. I snuck out and knocked Toma up, but he wasn't having it, so I walked up towards the top shops and bought a bottle of red lemonade. I drank it down in one sup, counted to ten then ended up on my hunkers emptying my body of everything that I had taken in.

Crawling up along the side of the church, I hoped the world would go away. The wind was torture. I held on to my cap, passing a line of beer crates stacked in line against the wall. In the corner of my eye I spotted Charlie standing about five feet away. His gang were like commandos as they came over the wall.

He was one of ten brothers and it was widespread news that he slept on the floor in the sittingroom. His gangs were made up of pickpockets and housebreakers; they were a rough faced untidy bunch.

"Here Twinny, what are yah doing up here?" he shouted as I walked closer.

I held on to my cap with one hand, pulled up the collar of my jacket with the other. Then I turned away from the wind and lit up a cigarette.

"Stay down the South, do yah hear me?"

"Snap out of it. Who are you, lord over Finglas? I go where I like," I snarled back.

The morning had grown darker, inside the church the boys in the white dresses ripped in to a chorus of 'Jesus is King, he is Lord of all the earth'. Their voices seemed to pierce the colorful glass above us. There was a short pause and then I heard the bells.

"Here, Charlie! Punch holes in 'em," a small kid roared, standing with his back against the wall, while paring a stick with a pen-knife. The cap he wore was that big I imagined we could all stand under it if the rain came.

I could hear the man of the cloth shouting; "*Go into the world, from the back alleys to the open fields and invite them to come to the wedding feast.*"

Charlie threw a punch, I slid under it and caught him with a right hook. I jumped back with my fist clenched. The boys, who all had their sleeves rolled up, circled me.

"Right Twinny, ye've had it now," Charlie said, as he climbed up from the ground.

Suddenly a voice that was filled with anger roared behind me. "There yah are Charlie, yah cabbage."

I moved to the side not taking my eyes off the rough wild boys. I saw a youth of my own age running down the lane. He kicked over the crates, sending a group of wild pigeons into the air. The choirboys continued to sing, the youth ran, and Charlie lost about a stone when he saw the Bulldog of a boy coming towards him. He wasn't alone either. Other boys closed both sides of the lanes off.

The Bulldog was dressed like Rocky in a grey track-suit with a hood on the back. The sound of bongo drums coming from the radio of a parked car floated down the lane.

"Here dance to that," I said to the boys who suddenly lost their appetite for a Sunday scrap.

The Bull Dog was walking close, breathing heavily. I could see by his face that he hadn't been at mass for a very long time.

"Who are yah calling a stocking?" he screamed at Charlie, who, before he could say an act of contrition, received about four blows to the head.

The angelic voices hit a feverish pitch sailing into the world of the bad boys; it fell into rhythm with the sound of the bongo drums. "Hallelujah, Hallelujah, the Lord is Master, where sin abounds, grace abounds all the more."

The Bulldog turned on Charlie's mates, punching two or three of them full force into the face. Then he turned on Charlie again who was now lying on the ground.

A priest in a flowing robe sailed around the corner. He stopped in the middle of the boys at the top of the lane. Bull Dog gave him one look baptizing him in a river of fear. He backed off and so did I, but before I did, I walked back to the little kid and snatched the knife from his hand.

"Little boys shouldn't play with big boys toys. Now go home and help your ma carry some coal in with your cap."

When I looked behind me, I saw three boys running down the lane with sledge hammers. I jumped over the wall. I waited for a few moments for them to reappear, but they didn't.

I tossed a coin into the air. "Heads she loves me, harps she doesn't," I whispered, as the coin twirled in the morning sky. A breeze caught the coin changing its direction. And as quickly as the coin turned so would time move for those boys. By the time a decade had passed not one of them would be alive.

I watched the coin spin and fall. Unfortunately, it landed on harps.

"What's the story?" Johnny Fitz shouted from a passing car. I waved and walked on down the street. Franko stuck his head around the wall.

"I saw Nicky and Mousey being chased by the police. They won't catch them, Twinny, I'm never wrong, catch yah later," Franko said before rushing across the street.

I wanted to cross over onto the wide path that many walked on. But the wind from heaven was so forceful it blew me onto a narrow path and I walked alone. Franko was wrong, they were caught and I never did see him again. His ma found him bent over in the toilet with a needle in his arm.

Nicky will reached the grand old age of twenty-eight, and

when he does, a bullet will send him to an early grave. Mousy will die screaming.

Drugs, the good life, maybe Nick, Mousy, Franko and so many others missed the good part. The grave is a hungry beast that's never full.

I was very worried about the coin and why it didn't turn in my favour. Then I thought about ma and da. They knew I came in late so that worried me even more.

Ma blew the pages of her book when I entered the kitchen. I could smell the Sunday roast. She gave me a look that could cut you in two; I didn't move. I just stood there feeling like I was around the same size as Action Man. Before she said anything, the door opened and in walked da.

"This is a home, not a hotel," he said, while placing his bike under the stairs.

"What time did you get in at?" he asked with a cross look.

"I don't know, da."

"I am telling yah, George, I don't give a crap about whose doing what. But one thing I'll tell yah, yah wouldn't want to come to this house in that state again and yah can tell the Joseph fella that as well."

"Sorry Da, sorry Ma," I said as I left the room.

After dinner I decided to lose myself in the Sunday matinee. I felt very comfortable sitting at the fire. Ma brought me over a cup of coffee. Little Wesley played on the carpet in front off me. A thought crossed my mind while sitting on the armchair. She had made no attempt to phone. Not even a single note.

I saw the full picture. She had met someone else, probably that Tim fella. Her parents would approve of him. I was convinced that this sudden flare of wisdom which crossed my mind was accurate.

I sat right back and rested my feet on the small table. It was an October evening. The darkness seemed to hover all around me.

I stared into space and thought about the day we went for a walk and I thought about how awkward I'd felt. Everything about the day lingered in my mind, the smells of the open field, the leaves, the grass, the fresh fragrance of wild flowers and the perfume she wore.

I imagined the little house in the distance was ours and then my heart sank because I remembered how the wind blew her hair and her eyes sparkled and I wondered if I had kissed her would she have been offended.

I stared at the coffee, my eyes felt tired. Sleep was drawing near, my head was nodding, eyes closing, can't hold on, I am drifting, heaviness is here, eyes closed... gone.

The first question I asked when I woke was, "Did anyone ring, Ma?"

"No," she replied.

I jumped up, took a hot bath, followed by a shave. I got dressed and splashed on some of da's aftershave. It stung a bit. I went into the kitchen, made a cup of coffee, drank it down in two sups, raced out the door, and grabbed a taxi.

"Where to?" the driver asked.'

"O'Connell Street, please."

The car drove down Rathvilly Park, across Cardiff Bridge down into the South. It turned the corner as we headed for the city. I stared out the window. Light snow was beginning to fall. The streets and garden walls were coated in white.

The inside of the taxi had a mixture of smells lodged between tobacco and aftershave.

My heart skipped a beat. There she was walking alone. She was wearing a light blue duffel coat, her hair neatly pulled down at the sides.

"Pull over here please."

"What! I thought you said town."

"Yeah well forget that," I replied, handing him a fiver.

The car pulled up on to the path. I could see my reflection in the mirror; I was wearing a black leather jacket and white tee-shirt with a little gold chain.

I jumped out and my boots made a crackling sound as the snow spread beneath them. I mustered up enough courage and then called her. She was a good distance off so I called again. She glanced over her shoulder but kept walking.

"How are yah doing, Sandra?" a group of youths said as they passed. She smiled but kept going until she just disappeared up the lane.

When I reached the lane she was walking backwards with her long coat pulled tightly around her, her hands buried deep into her pockets. The high heel shoes she wore gave her height and maturity.

"Where's a boy like you going on a cold night like this?" she asked, while her eyes remained still and sensual.

"Just out looking for a friend," I replied, staring deeply into her eyes that dazzled like jewels under the night sky.

"Yah won't find many friends in back lanes," she said, commanding each word carefully.

I was seeing her for the first time. Behind the soft spoken shy girl was a very confident person that had no desire to flaunt her strength to the world.

"Yah need to be careful, walking along these lanes on your own," I said, slowly advancing towards her.

"Who said I'm on my own. From where I'm standing, I can see a boxer."

She stopped and leaned against the wall. I stretched across her and rested my hand on the black wall. A mother called her son from the back window. A police siren could be heard in the distance, but the noise from the street couldn't touch us. Minutes passed between us but neither of us spoke.

I ran my fingers along her soft face, my heart throbbing, then our lips touched and we kissed. I put my arms around her; she leaned back while I held her in a full tight grip. I caught hold of her hand, held it tightly and then kissed each finger.

"Come on," I said as I grabbed her and we ran through the back lanes and alleys.

I looked towards the lane. Boys were gathered on the corner drinking.

"All right Georgie?" Gazer shouted as we passed.

"Nice one Gaz," I shouted back.

"How are we going to keep this a secret?" she asked, her voice filled with innocence. "What are we going to do George?"

"That's very simple. Goatee believes that if you're invisible you can take anything you want, so from now on I am invisible."

I took her hand and we ran again hand in hand laughing, until we found a dark corner. I reached forward till our lips touched and we kissed again. It seemed to last forever. Her face was cold from the night air. We held each other as we stood in the darkness for a long time.

"Now listen," I said. "See those streets - they watch everything. What you don't say they can't hear."

And that's how we lived - in secret.

The snow lit up the lane as we stood arm in arm. I turned towards Gazer and the boys who were standing on the corner.

"Here Gazer look," I said, pointing heavenwards, the moon sparkling in the night sky. "Someone up there likes me too."

Sandra and I spent the first few years of our courtship in secret. But by the time she reached the grand old age of sixteen, it was official and we could be seen together in public.

ROUND 20

Joe, Pat, and I sat watching 'Swap Shop' one Saturday morning. Up until now we had spent every waking moment dreaming about becoming boxing champions. Since we had stopped boxing, a lack of vision in our lives had left a gap.

"Here Joe! What will we do next?" I asked.

"What about going to see UB40 in the Stadium on Friday night," Pat said.

"I don't mean that. I mean, like, wha' will we do, like, to become famous?"

Joe was working in Pearse Street in a brassfoundry at the time.

"I have it," he said jumping off the chair. "We'll make gold rings out of brass and sell them for a pound a pop."

"Yeah all we have to do is sell a million," I replied.

"What about UB40?" Pat asked again.

"What about them?" Joe and I said together.

"Will we go and see them on Friday or wha'?"

"Yeah, we'll sell the rings at the gig," I shouted.

"I don't think I'll make a million by Friday," Joe replied.

The Stadium was packed when we arrived. The music pumped out from the speakers and we joined in with the dancing crowd. When UB40 took to the stage the place went wild; they were awesome. Joe got a bit exited and jumped up on the stage and pulled the mike out of Ali Campbell's hand. We gave out a big cheer as he did a little dance and ran. But the roadies caught him and lifted him back down over the barriers.

When we got on the bus after the gig, we were on a high and we talked about all the different bands. I said that UB40 were the best band in the world. Toma said Madness were better. Joe wondered what it would be like to be in a band. I said, "Why don't we start our own band?" Pat said, "That is a brilliant idea."

The three of us walked around the back bedroom that night thinking about a name for the band.

"I know - UB2O," Pat shouted.

"That's crap," I replied.

Pat came back with, "What about 'The UB Runaways'?"

"That sounds like a Hillbilly band," Joe said.

"The Finglas Runaways then," Pat shouted.

"Na Pat. 'The Forty Runaways', 'Runners Doing Forty'."

"Here, will yah give it up or I'll be doin' a runner," I said.

"That's it, Runner," they said.

"Right, I'll keep saying names and when one sticks, you say that's it. Right."

"Right."

"The Finglas Runners...The Dublin City Runners...The Dublin Runners... The Dublin 11 Runners...The D11Runners."

"That's it. 'The D11 Runners'."

We went to bed that night happy because not only were we starting a band but now we had a name, 'The D11 Runners'.

We were very happy about the name, now all we had to do was recruit band members, save a fortune, buy the instruments, learn to play, find a manager, play gigs, and sell singles, make a million. No problem.

We had a meeting in Weller's the following Friday night. We decided that the line-up of the band should be the same as UB40. Joe suggested that we pull names out of a hat to find out what instruments we would play. My name came out with saxophone.

Joe, Pat, Weller, Paulo, and I spent the next few months talking about the band. But I was beginning to wonder whether it was ever going to happen at all. Because all we did was argue about who was going to do TV and radio interviews! It then got to a stage where we began whispering like we were FBI agents just in case anyone heard about it and robbed our idea.

The June bank holiday weekend arrived. I was sitting on the couch in the sittingroom with the window opened. It was a beautiful day. Ma and da were gone away for the weekend, they brought Wesley with them. I saw Joe and Pat turn the corner with a gang following hot on their heels.

"Right, George, I have the band," Joe said as he and Pat and about ten boys marched in behind them.

"Brilliant!" I replied, jumping off the chair and dashing into the kitchen and out to the backgarden. When I returned I brought back sweeping brushes, yard brushes, and shovels.

"Here Pat, you get the pots," Joe said.

So we separated the boys that had guitars, meaning brushes to one side of the room, while the others sat on the floor acting as fans. Joe lifted a hairbrush to his mouth and took a deep breath. Pat put on the sounds. Everyone waited and Joe roared "Let's Rock The Shop."

I swung my guitar into the air, it nearly smashed the light. Joe did a Michael Jackson twirl roaring: "Yeah man, the big time is just in front of us."

I dived on the floor and smacked Mick, right on the nose. Pat shouted over, "That's brilliant George - slapping the pots that hard, he nearly rubbed the steel off them.

"Thanks Pat, yah know what? We're going to make it."

"Without a doubt," Joe said breathlessly.

After the jam we drank down long glasses of lemonade and

talked about how we were going to divide the money up. But that conversation led to an argument because some of the boys were trying to say that we were ripping them off.

After they left, I turned to Joe and said:

"Here, your man Dave is out of the band. Right. He comes into our gaff, drinks all the lemonade, and says I'm rippin' him off. Oh by the way, Pat yah were brilliant on the pots."

"Thanks. I always knew I had it in me."

"I think you're a natural," Joe replied.

"By the way if we are going to be serious about this, tell the boys the next time we jam, to bring their own brushes," I said.

"Yeah it looks thick passing them around," Pat replied.

That night I met Sandra and told her that my days working for a living were nearly over! That Saturday I closed my credit union account. The woman called me into the office and asked me how I came to this quick decision.

I tipped my cap back, lifted the front leg of the chair and said, "This time next year I'm going to be a millionaire."

We saved up and bought our first guitar. The man in the shop gave us a small piece of plastic, he said it was called a plectrum. Joe carried the guitar, Pat carried the amp, and I carried the plectrum.

"Here you carry the amp and I'll carry the black thumb," Pat said as we walked along Parnell Street.

"It's not a black thumb. The man said, it's a plectrum."

"Show me it, show me it."

"Here," I said, handing it to him.

He placed the amp down, took the plectrum and started to clean his nails.

"Now do yah get it, black thumb. It's for cleaning your nails so yah don't dirty the strings."

"Jayney, man, they think of everything," I said.

That night Weller came up to the house to show us how to turn the amp on. When the red light came on, I looked to my brothers and said, "It's only a matter of time before we make it."

When 1986 arrived, we had formed a real band. Joe was the lead singer, Pat played trumpet, while Sandra and I played saxophone. Jackie - Joe's girlfriend - played bass, Weller played keyboards, and Paulo was on the drums.

We began to work the northside playing in all the rundown pubs. I wrote false reviews and signed them using a fake name. Then we got posters printed and blanked the city with them. We phoned 'Hot Press' magazine and 'In Dublin' pretending that we were fans, asking for information on the band, in the hope that they would come to see us. It was around this time that our name began to appear in the paper and the pirate radio stations started to play our demo tapes.

And by the time 1988 had arrived, we had developed a strong name as an up and coming band.

Sandra was growing; I felt that she should try and branch into modelling. So after much persuading, she finally agreed to take part in a photo shoot that I had arranged. When I got the portfolio, I posted them around the city to different agencies.

One Monday night she received a phone call from an agency on the southside. She started the following Wednesday and worked through the summer finishing the course. But when the winter came she stopped going, she said she hated it. The agency rang and rang but she stopped taking their calls and they finally gave up. So Sandra spent her days working in a factory in Finglas and her nights playing gigs.

At that time I was assigned to a construction gang who were working on the basement of an old house on the docklands. Plastering jobs became scarce so when the plastering was finished the foreman gave me a shovel, just so he could keep me on.

The band continued to grow in the underground scene. We booked out the Ivy Rooms on Parnell Street and packed it night after night. Then we moved across the Liffey and started to pack out the famous, Baggot Inn, where the likes of U2 and Thin Lizzy had made their names.

The horn rang on the site. I dropped the shovel and jumped out of the trench. It was a beautiful hot day. I kept walking while pulling my jumper off and tying it around my waist. Tipping my cap back as the sun had coloured my shoulders a dark brown. I looked up along the quays and spotted Joe rushing towards me.

"What's happenin'?" I asked before he reached me.

"Loads. We got an interview on two small radio stations on Tuesday night, and Peter our manager has got a meeting with Louis Walsh on Monday."

"Louis Walsh, he's a showband manager isn't he?"

"Yeah, but he's not into that anymore. Oh, we have a new guitarist, his name is Ken Mc Cluskey, he lives in Finglas down the south."

"Do we get to meet this Louis guy or what?"

"Yeah, he told Peter that there's a Don Baker gig on next Saturday and he'll try to get us on for about a half hour set."

We've got to make it, yah know what I mean. I'm down a hole digging, look at me hands."

"Yah, want to see what I'm doing. It's a load of crap."

But listen, this Louis bloke could help us. He told Peter that he had heard rumours going around that Alan Parker is making a movie about bands in Ireland sometime next year. He said if it comes off, he will try to get us on it.

"Alan Parker!"

"Yeah, he made Fame, Midnight Express, Bugsy Malone and loads more."

"They were good films," I said.

"Listen, I'd better get back or the wardens at Sing Sing will have a search party out looking for me," I then said.

"If we get that gig, I'll ring yah tonight. OK."

Joe and Jackie had married, by this time he was no longer living at home. He rang like he said he would and we got the gig.

The Saturday came. I placed the mouthpiece of the saxophone between my teeth and blew into it. The sound filled the bell. Then it escaped into the night. A night that was cool and brightly lit up, by the silver stars and the glittering moon.

I climbed the steps that ran on the outside of the old red brick building, as the rattling sound of the band on stage billowed out of the open door.

I had stepped out to warm up before going on stage. I played the horn, running my finger along the polished buttons, moving it from octave to octave until the notes rang out chasing each other, touching a star and then vibrating into the lane below.

Silence accompanied the awaiting crowd. Smoke billowed out from the restaurant and rested under the blue and amber lights that lined the streets. It hovered at the feet of the crowd as damp wind rushed in, hurrying the dirt and grime along as if it had no earthly business being there in the first place.

I glanced over the skyline with my head covered in a white slick bandana that was capped in a porcupine hat. I saw a cat helping himself to dinner. A window of a nearby flat opened. A bald-headed man stuck his head out dressed in a dirty tee-shirt. His window-ledge was covered in empty beer cans. I watched him pick one up and fire it across the flat rooftop. The side door opened. The cat ran and Joe called me: "Are yah right? We're up next."

His words carried a memory and for the smallest of moments, the tiniest of seconds, I thought that Rocky or Danny might make an appearance. I followed him down along the spiral staircase, zig-zagging in and out between managers, roadies and long legged girls.

When we reached our band, they were lined up at the back of the stage. I pulled back the curtain and saw the audience standing upright covering every inch of the floor, their necks stiff and their hands filled with pints.

The first support band finished. The stage became empty. Then we descended onto the platform to the smell of beer that was married to the heavy scent of wine.

The long hours of rehearsals combined with the smiles that celebrated our arrival was truly rewarding. But everything hinges on a moment that is not rehearsed. It sneaks in; there's no guarantee that it will happen, but when it does, all the stars shine down on you. And a moment arrives that can't be matched by the greatest of fairytales. We were stars in the making, money makers from the word go, and we knew it.

The inner city club rang out with a tremendous applause as we charged from one song into another, paving the way for our instrumental that spring boarded us into Joe's solo. But as quickly as a picture on the TV is reduced to a dot, our set came to an end and we left the stage to the applause of the satisfied crowd.

Chairs were set out for us as drinks were handed down. Sandra rose from the chair and crossed the floor, her long legs moved with grace. She passed the stage and when she returned, the silver haired man took the centre.

Don Baker picked up the harmonica, placed it to his mouth, and spoke through each note, before moving it from a melodic haunting sound, to an experience, until a vision lay before you. The greatest harmonica player this country has ever known.

When he finished the crowd were ecstatic, the pints were pouring, and the autograph seekers surrounded him. He smiled over, then left us to bathe in the new experience. We were now in the world of fast clothes, fast money, and even fast talkers.

Joe sat back and looked at a bald headed man. He withdrew his eyes and stole another look and when he did he noticed that the man was studying him. My attention was arrested when I noticed a small man standing at the bar. When the bald headed man saw that he had caught our attention, he rose from his seat and approached us. Screwing up his nose, he introduces himself as Rizzo.

Rizzo stared down at the glass and reached for a chair. Our faces became flushed, as a great swirl of bodies surrounded us, rich kids, slick talkers, ladies and gentlemen who spoke with a twang.

I stared across the floor thinking I know that man's face. I stood up and slid by the sweat-soaked mob and headed for the bar. The sound of the crowd echoed in the background as two dancers that seemed to melt in each others arms bumped off me.

When the man at the bar came into focus I recognized him. Twelve years or so had past but I still remembered him. He was the little mousey faced kid that stood in the lane with Snookerball. Another roar filled our ears as a stream of men lined the bar for last drinks.

"All right Twin?"

"Yeah, what's the story?"

I ordered us a drink.

"Do yah remember that yoke?" he asked while swallowing his pint.

"Yeah" I replied, staring at the picture above my head.

He drew closer to the bar and rested his pint. I withdrew my eyes. He turned around. I stole a look and noticed his lip was curved. The drink, the history shared and soft music that danced out of the speakers was enough to make anyone feel a little melancholy.

"I hope yah make it - Twin."

"Here. Three little boys went down that lane. Two of them are here to tell the tale, we did make it."

We shook hands, swallowed the pints and I headed back to my seat.

"We can help yah," I overheard Rizzo saying as I sat down.

He told us he had his own record company that was based in Dublin. We disguised our excitement while we met his gaze. Joe spoke with him, nothing was arranged, but we did plan to meet him once we got back from Spain.

There was a bright sun in the sky, the brightest I'd ever seen as I awoke on the coast of Spain during that summer of '87. I showered and walked out onto the balcony and watched the white waves that tried to invade the beach while the beautiful Spanish girls cleaned the tables below me.

"Good morning, Madame," I shouted, dancing to the morning music. Then I dressed and went down to the breakfast bar. Twenty of us were holidaying together that year. Most of us were stood at the bar that morning.

"Poarlez vous francaise," I said to Sandra.

"That's French, George. We're in Spain."

"Yeah, well, all those foreigners sound the same. Here, let's have breakfast somewhere else," I said nudging her in the ribs.

"I'll hire a bike, and we'll head off somewhere nice."

When no one was looking we both crept away and headed for the bike shop.

She closed her eyes and held on as we whizzed past the side

walk and travelled along the main road, set in palm trees with beautiful rows of flowers.

In front was a narrow road that led up to a mountain, the type you would see in a spaghetti western. A light breeze blew as I went up the hill at full speed. When we got to the top, we left the bike, took off our sandals, and went for a walk.

I looked down on the flat-roofed apartments. Birds covered the roof of a little kiosk. The waves crashed against the arched landscape. I stood in the bright sun, staring down at the picturesque view, with the rugged mountain in the background and Sandra by my side.

"I know what James Cagney meant when he said, "Ma, I'm on top of the world."

"It's always the gangster, you're just about to make a romantic statement and up pops James Cagney," she said, lightly punching me in the arm.

"Jimmy Cagney wasn't a gangster, he was an actor."

"So it's Jimmy now, yah know him that well."

"Ah relax. Here look at that," I said pointing to an even more beautiful view.

We sat there for what must have been an hour doing nothing but staring at the white waves and seagulls. I could smell the sea as I took in a deep lungful of air. The moment was calm and romantic.

"Here, Sandra, will we get married soon?"

"Do yah really want me to answer that?"

"Yeah."

She paused, "Promise yah won't be angry."

"I'm already angry."

"I am too young and so are you."

"You're eighteen. I am twenty-two... that's not young."

"I am too young," she said the second time, narrowing her eyes.

I swallowed hard and went to speak, she placed her finger over my lips and said, "Lets not spoil the day."

She stood up and walked across the remote hills. I watched her. Every movement oozed sensuality. She was perfection with her long black hair, chocolate brown shoulders, and deep ocean blue eyes.

"So what are you saying, I'm mad or something?"

"No relax, don't be so paranoid."

"Are you running away now, Sandra?"

"No I'm just making sure the bike is still there."

I jumped up and grabbed her from behind, gently whispering in her ear.

"Will you marry me someday?"

"What are yah rushing me for," she said sharply.

I walked away and sat back down.

"What's wrong?"

"Nothing."

She reached for my hand. I pulled it away.

"Come on, let's get something to eat."

"My appetite is gone," I said, sighing heavily.

She reached again for my hand, her fingers gently touched mine, and a soft shudder ran through me.

"Of course I will, but you'll just have to wait. OK."

As we drove into the town, the scenic view vanished. The wide sea front was replaced by small winding streets that opened up into a square. There were cafés everywhere that rolled out onto the streets. We ordered two English breakfasts.

"Come on, lets get out of here," I said after we finished breakfast. So we jumped on the bike and headed off. We found a beautiful beach, parked the bike and sat on the sand, watching the day come to a close.

Dark clouds covered the horizon. The sun began to fall into the sea. But it gave one more blast, breaking through the clouds, lighting up the earth until it fell on a dome church in the distance. The light flickered, the clouds gathered, and God sent a wind to blow it out, and the darkness came.

"Let's go for a drink."

"No sir, Mr Fitzgerald, I am not dressed for that. We'll go back and get changed first."

"Come on, no one knows yah. Look! There's a nice bar," I said, walking up the stone steps.

"Oh, OK, one drink - that's it."

I pushed the large doors of the restaurant open. Inside were marble columns that supported the most magnificent plastered ceiling I had ever seen. Large arched windows looked out onto the harbour.

The man brought us over to the table and sat us down.

"You're dreaming again."

"Sorry."

"What are you thinking of?"

"The book."

"The one you read?" she asked, placing her chin into her hand.

"Yeah."

"What are you're thoughts?"

"Rubbish. According to the writer, he states that Jesus was married, had children and then lived in France."

"Everything is plausible how do you know that what he is saying is not true?"

"He wasn't there. And neither was I. After two thousand years, it's a bit late in the day to be listening to that crap."

"After this drink, I'm going up to that church."

"Do you really want my opinion on that?"

"Well yah said only one drink, so let's purge ourselves of the impurities of the flesh."

"Don't be so melodramatic, let's just go back to the others."

"Anything yah say dear."

I pushed the doors open. Sandra followed. The entryway breathed out mystery. I stood in silence scanning the white walls and the dark chamber. I gazed at the images of Christ hanging above the lighted candles.

"What are we doing here?" Sandra asked, eyeing me strangely.

"I don't know," I whispered.

There was an inscription on the base of the cross written in Spanish. Underneath it were English words covered in dust. I walked toward Jesus. Looked around, fell to my knees, ran my hand across the inscription, and blew gently. The words came into focus: *If you search for me with all your heart, there you will find me.*

I fell back and stared at the words then I jumped to my feet, grabbed Sandra's hand and ran. As we sat on the bike I looked back at the church. I turned the key and drove off as fast as I could.

The holiday came to an end. We boarded the plane and headed for Dublin. But I never forgot those words, they stayed with me for a long time.

When we arrived back in Dublin Airport the first thing I did was pick up the phone and ring Sonny's house because we had arranged to meet him in the village for a drink.

"What's the story with Sonny?" Joe asked when I put the phone down

"He's gone on his own holiday," I said.

"We'll go up to see him in a week or so," Joe said as we left the airport.

ROUND 21

Sonny's situation was indeed one that was common to his wayward life, but despite this, my mind began to busy itself with the order of events that had befallen him.

I pondered along these lines as I walked towards the bus stop not long after I'd returned home from Spain. I saw Anto standing with one hand in his pocket and the other resting against the bus stop. He was thin, square-jawed and the hair that graced his head dropped down along his back. It was thick and black like that of a horse's mane. The long coat he wore dragged along the ground while he eyed everyone that moved within inches of him.

"How's it going, Twin? What's the Jackin'-ory?"

The wind whipped across us, blowing his hair across his face.

"I'm going up to see Sonny."

"I was in court when he got sentenced; sure I got a week in custody me-self."

While we waited on the bus he told me the whole story. The courtroom was small, the judge was not, neither was he impressed with the young man that stood before him. But Sonny was never one to be too concerned about what the little fat man said. His posture revealed that.

He stood with one hand on the polished timber while the other one remained in his pocket. He turned his head and looked around the court, fixing his eyes on the walls and benches. They were covered in faces that peered out from tight woolen hats and damp rain coats.

Then he set his gaze on the judge, who wasted no time in placing his glasses on while he stared down on the young man.

From the time the case began Sonny switched and turned, winked, and smiled, moving his hands and feet so much that the Judge thought at any moment he might break into a dance.

Then Sonny's mind entered into a tireless search of knowledge. He wondered what the judge had eaten for breakfast, he wondered what his father had eaten for breakfast, then he wondered if his ma had bought those cakes he liked and he wondered how long it would be before he ate them again. Suddenly his mind became instantly aware of where he was.

The noise of the talkers suddenly subsided to a hush as the Judge rang out the sentence of two years, then his recommendation came.

"You have appeared before me since a boy, yet in all my years I have not seen such a careless attitude from a lad. So I call you a hopeless case. And a face I have no doubt I will see a lot more of in the future. Take him down."

Only the sound of coughing could be heard as he was led down the stairs toward the holding cells under the court.

He quickly cleared the narrow steps, a garda leading the way. He opened one door and brought him through another.

"Move back," shouted the guard as the key turned in the cell door. The door opened and Sonny was pushed in. In the corner was a boy who wore laceless boots and clothes as dirty as a coal man.

"The van will be here soon to take us to the Joy. I hope we don't miss the grub, yah know what I mean."

Sonny never replied, he just sat there waiting on the van to arrive.

When Anto had finished giving me his first hand account of Sonny's dilemma, the one that Sonny had given him. I got on the bus and said nothing all the way into town. But I did slip into Gardiner Street church to say a little prayer for the boys.

When I walked out, I met a priest we had known as boys.

"How're yah Paul?" We always called him by his first name.

"How are yah?" he said.

I told him about Sonny.

"I'll say a prayer for him," he said.

"Here say a prayer for us. We're playing a big gig next week."

"I will Georgie son," he said as I dashed over the puddles, holding on to my cap as I headed for home.

His feet were dancing, his shoes were tapping, and the young man had a voice like an angel. He spun on his heels under the revolving light as the flaps of his shirt flew on the wings of the wind.

The onlooking crowd fell into a trance, when my twin brother reached a high note. It was as if the celestial beings had come down to join him in a heavenly chorus. The crowds were mesmerized. Even our band that stood behind the curtain experienced a tingling feeling. His voice had captured the moment and the hearts of the people; it was a significant turn around, a showcase that carried a powerful statement which said, 'The D11 Runners were a force to be reckoned with."

Silence filled the air as his last note thundered through the atmosphere. This brought about a standing ovation even before the band played their first song. He turned towards us when we walked behind the curtain, dressed in a white shirt and a peakless cap.

"Right lets play a stormer," he said, as the nightclub fell into darkness.

We took our positions, and waited for the command of the overseeing officer. Paulo shouted, one, two, three, four. The sound of the saxophones, trumpets, and keyboards, combined with our colourful image of caps, bandanas, minis, and braces, hit the crowd like a bolt of lightning, electrifying them into a frenzied state as the smoke from the machine rose up. And the lights went on plunging us out of the darkness into a blazing fire of glory.

Everything was moving very fast, the crowds were growing, tee-shirts and caps were being sold at the gigs, but the most important part for us was that the music was beginning to get tighter.

In the middle of the set our younger brother Pat would move from behind his percussion and take the spotlight with his dance routine. He was learning to motivate the crowd masterfully. He would move on cue, dressed like a bull fighter with his red bandanna that had gold spots spread across it. His black trousers had a high waist and the shoes he wore shone in the light. His shirt front would swing wildly, revealing his tight midsection that was covered in perspiration.

The audience cheered as he flew into mid-air, landing perfectly as if to the command of a conductor. He was like us, self-taught, but his dancing was so impressive that in the years to come Louis Walsh, our agent would ask him to audition for a new band he had in mind called Boyzone. But he declined the offer with thanks.

Halfway through the set, I reached down for a glass of water and that's when I noticed Goatee. He was in the front of the crowd, standing with my friend Toma. My heart was overjoyed. I hadn't seen him in five years. Naturally he looked older, he had grown into a big man, but that boyish look still hovered around him.

I walked underneath the spotlight and played a solo, as Paulo lightly brushed the drums with his feathered brushes. The notes echoed through the air, slicing the atmosphere. Beads of sweat broke out across my forehead. But I turned my mind to yesterday, and remembered the boy, with the dirty brown hair and long legs. And the cold winters day when he pulled back the timber planks that ran between the old red brick wall. He reached into the gap and pulled out a small bag of money.

"Here do yah want a few quid?" he asked with a grin.

"No thanks, Goatee," I replied, as I watched him stuff it beneath the insoles of his well worn shoe, jump on a bike and head up the road waving. It was the last time I saw him until tonight.

The bass drum was beating, a sea of people, were moving in rhythm, waving their hands in the air. As the set came to an end, we walked behind the curtain. The clamour of voices crying out for an encore was a song in itself. Joe ran out behind the curtain, the band followed suit and once again exploded out of the darkness. For us, in that moment, this was what life was all about.

After the gig we sat in the dressing room, the door opened and Tony St Ledger walked in. Tony was a tall dark and handsome man who had a brilliant mind. When it came to music, he was right behind the band. With only one thing on his mind: "Get the sounds right man and everything will follow."

Later, I got a chance to talk to Goatee in the midst of signing autographs and claps on the back from men who were dressed like Bono and long-legged girls who wore smiling faces. We stood at the bar and talked about the five years that passed. The good news was he was now married, and held down a good job.

When we stepped out onto the streets, the rain was beginning to fall. It was time for each of us to go our separate ways again.

We embraced then he ran across the bridge. I shouted after him, "Goatee, I am proud of yah."

"Don't be, remember you were the fighter brother. I just hope I go all the way," he added.

"Just keep going, remember the opera's not over, until the fat lady sings, just keep going," I said.

I never did meet him again, after that night, but I believe he's doing well.

May the sun always shine down on you, my friend...

The year 1989 started off with a bang. Sandra and I were planning on getting married the following year. We were also planning on buying our first house in South Finglas. But a friend of ours died tragically at the age of twenty-two.

I can remember watching the coffin being lowered into the ground, listening intently to the priest recite the famous 23rd psalm, The Lord is my Shepherd. I watched the grave being filled in and the crowd move away. I walked awkwardly behind with my hands in my pockets not knowing what to say. I just kept walking until I ended up sitting on a hill at the back of the slaughter house. My head was full of questions. We had known a lot of boys and young men who had died over the years, but now I wanted answers. Sonny once told me that while he was locked up, he read the bible. I thought he was mad. But somehow on that day it was the only thing that seemed to make any sense. So I decided that as soon as I could I was going to buy a bible.

The rain was pouring down as I reached the city centre the following Saturday. I pulled my jacket around my neck and hurried past the traffic and the afternoon shoppers. I grimaced as the rain swept across my face while standing at the end of

O'Connell Street waiting for the traffic lights to change.

When I finally reached Bachelors Walk, I entered a small book shop that sold Bibles. There was a huge stack of Bibles and other commentaries on the ancient book. Behind the counter stood a heavyset man. He looked over the rim of his glasses at me. I could see he was somewhat uncomfortable with my presence. I felt a bit clumsy and out of place standing there in my long coat, hoody, and tight black monkey hat.

"Do you sell Bibles?" I asked, in a shop that sold nothing else.

"Full marks for observation," the old man said in an English accent.

Does he think I'm a dope or something? I thought.

"What version are you looking for?"

"The one that," I paused for a moment, "the one that tells the story about Ben Hur."

"I'm afraid that version hasn't been printed yet," he said, smiling.

What's the story with that oul fella? I thought. I could see he hadn't a clue about the Bible, so I gave him a lesson in the shop. I told him how Jesus rescued Ben Hur's family as the blood poured from the cross and healed them, and when I had finished, he told me quite plainly that the story of Ben Hur was purely fictional. He also said that it was not recorded in the Holy Scripture. I paused for a moment before pointing to a Bible.

"How much is that one?"

"Nine pound" he said while standing beside me. The bell over the door rang and in walked a little woman. The shopkeeper quickly attended her.

"How much is that one?" I replied, pointing to the one with NIV on the front.

"Four ninety five," he quickly said, while turning back toward the old lady.

"Right, here, nice one," I said. I handed him the money and walked out.

"Your receipt," he shouted.

"Don't worry, stick the money in your pocket," I shouted back with a wink.

When I looked in the window the man and the woman were praying.

That oul one must have problems, I thought.

I crossed the street, stood outside a record shop and glanced in the window. My thoughts of stardom were interrupted when I bumped into Weller and his girlfriend.

"Here we have a meeting arranged for tomorrow night. We need to talk about the single."

"I reckon we've got a big hit on our hands. Listen, I'm in a rush. Joe can fill me in when I get home. I'll catch you later," I said as I walked off and headed for the bus stop.

The meeting place was a hotel in the inner city. The floor was set in black and white marble tiles. Pictures that looked like old books hung from the walls. The fireplace was open and warmly smoldering the room.

Weller stood sipping his pint while he looked all around the place.

"Will yah sit down," Pat shouted.

"I was just thinking, there's no way, anyone is going to order any of our singles," he said, placing his pint on the table.

"Hold on; let's look at it for a moment," Joe replied, as he leaned back on his chair. "So what Rizzo's telling us is, no one goes into the charts by sales, it's all about orders."

Everyone was surprised by this news.

"Yeah right. So who's going to order an unknown, unsigned

band's first single, when top acts like Phil Collins and George Michael have singles coming out at the same time?" Weller replied.

We all stared at him for a moment.

"Well that's my opinion," he added leaning back in the chair, lifting his pint off the table.

"Right we need two things: a plan and money. Once we have a good plan in place we'll crack the system," I said. "And here's the plan. "First we find a few small shops and buy the singles from there."

"How are we going to do that?" Pat asked.

"A brown envelope will sort that out."

"What do yah mean, a brown envelope?" Weller asked.

"We're going to have to pay," Joe replied.

"What I'm saying is. We'll get the shopkeeper to order say, about three hundred singles, right. We'll pay him in advance before he has them. So he has nothing to lose. Now who's going to turn down that sort of deal?" I said.

"Oh, I see, but what happens next?" Pat asked.

"Then we'll have spotters on the street. They'll go into the bigger shops to order and buy out the singles. And in the mean time, we'll order the single by phone," Joe added.

"So it looks like you already have it sorted," Weller said.

"There's only one problem," Pat said. "How will we know how many to buy each week?"

"That's sorted. We have a bloke on the inside who works in a record company. He'll ring us on a Thursday morning with all the figures we need," Joe again cut in.

"How'll we shift them?" Paulo asked.

"At the gigs. We're booked to play a lot of big clubs and there's a good chance we could get rid of three hundred a night," Joe added.

"But first, we have to get one or two blokes to ask the shopkeepers, if they're interested in the deal. No band members and no names. We don't want some bloke running around telling people that The D11 Runners are scamming it," I said.

"Right, Joe said, we'll have everything in place for Saturday morning."

We drank down our pints and left. The elevator was crammed so we took the stairs. We grabbed a taxi in O'Connell Street. The driver drove a bit crazy and we made Finglas in record time. We stood on the corner going over every detail again and again.

This was our only shot. We had to make sure that everything was in place. The following days were spent preparing for Saturday. It arrived quicker than expected, but when it did, we were ready.

ROUND 22

The sound of the busy streets were calmed when the doors of the inner city coffee shop closed behind us. Joe and I were wearing caps and grandfather shirts. Pat had a colourful bandana covering his head. We found a chair by the window and sat down. The hand on the large clock struck three as we sipped the coffee.

Two men dressed in long leather coats and baseball caps walked into a small record shop in Dublin city. We had hand picked these men. They were not band members. Under no circumstances were they to reveal the name of the band or the amount of singles we wanted the shopkeeper to order. This knowledge would be forthcoming once he'd received his first payment. If things went wrong the band would be finished and the shopkeeper would be in trouble.

After they talked with the owner, he called them into the room at the back of the shop. They shook hands and struck a deal. It was arranged that he would receive his first payment on Saturday week.

Suddenly our friends appeared outside the coffee shop. Both of them lit up a smoke and walked in. One of them, a small man who was dressed in a long coat, walked directly into the men's room. I got up and followed him, leaving my cigarette smouldering in the ashtray. I kept my foot up against the door as I pulled out a brown envelope.

"Well, what did he say?"

"It's cool. He'll take the money and order the singles."

"Right Andy, can we trust yah?"

"Yeah sure, yah can, I wouldn't rip yis off."

"Right, look into my eyes."

We stared at each other for a moment without blinking.

"Right pay him now," I said, as I handed him the envelope.

"He's not expecting the money until next week."

"Exactly, so pay him now. I'll see yah when we get home."

"Right, no problem, talk to yah then," he said, tucking the envelope into his pocket.

The reason for the advance payment was the brainchild of Paulo. If the shopkeeper took the money when he wasn't expecting us, he couldn't do anything when he was.

The leather chair made a creaking sound when I sat down. Before I lifted my cup, Joe spoke: "Can we trust him?"

"Yeah, there's no stealing in his eyes," I replied, while I took a drag on the cigarette.

"Right Pat, make that phone call."

He walked across the street, went into a phone box and asked the shopkeeper if he had got the money. He did. Andy could be trusted.

"Right boys, lets go, we have a gig to play," Pat shouted as he stuck his head round the door.

The sky was as blue as the Pacific Ocean with blistering rays of sun running through it as we walked onto the stage in the open-air gig outside the Central Bank. The crowds were waiting in anticipation for our arrival. The atmosphere was electric. We had just finished a tour with an international band called Technotronic who were fronted by MC Einstein and Melissa. Their hits included 'Pump up the Jam' and 'This Beat is Technotronic. During the tour, we also received rave reviews in a music magazine. A journalist wrote that the 'D11 Runners, went down a treat with the enthusiastic crowd, who were more than pleased when they performed'.

It wasn't funk and it wasn't disco, it was the sound of the northside that swam down to the crowd, and caught the paperboy on the corner and the taxi men who pulled over on that beautiful day in Dublin. The flashing lights and the roaring crowds made us feel like pop stars. We started off with a drum roll followed by the bass and then the brass section.

An American company flew over from New York to see the band play live. They were not part of the music business, nor had they got any interest in our musical ability. They were film makers, who wanted to make a cartoon that would run in competition with the Simpsons. The cartoon they had in mind was to be based in Dublin, with two Dublin brothers as the main characters. When they saw us and heard the sounds they loved us, so a deal was arranged. But the backers pulled out at the last minute.

After the open-air gig, we met Don Baker again. He asked Sandra if she would be interested in playing as a session worker in his band, but due to our busy schedule she declined.

The gig was wonderful. Ma, da and Wesley were in the crowd, so was Toma and the boys. I waved to them as we left the stage.

The sun shone in through the window as we made our way home, through the crowded streets, we were alive, big time.

The Daily Star ran a story on the band. The headline was: *On the Run to the Top*. The article, written by rock critic Eugene Masterson, featured a photo of Sandra, Joe and me. The article went on to state that the Alan Parker film, "The Commitments," based on Roddy Doyle's book, was inspired by us, after Roddy had seen the band. Eugene was a great help during a time when very few reporters took much notice of us. But now everyone was talking about the film and our connections from Gerry

Ryan to Gay Byrne. When we met Roddy Doyle his advice was, "Milk it boys as best you can."

Later on, Sandra and I walked through the neighbourhood and up along the lane to the place where we first kissed. The night was cold so we stood behind the wall, placing our hands in one another's pockets and pressing our bodies against each other.

"I have to meet Christy tomorrow. Then go and try my suit on. After that I have to meet Joe in town," I said.

"Don't forget, we have to go to the hotel tomorrow as well to arrange a few things."

"How could I forget that?" I said, grabbing her hand. "The days will shorten soon, but when they are, we will be married."

She placed her hand on my chest. "I can feel your heart beating," she said, resting her head in the same place. We kissed and I walked her to her gate and then disappeared into the night.

The next morning, I jumped up out of the bed. "Oh look at the time," I heard myself say as I pulled back the quilt and raced around the bedroom. I ran down the stairs fastening my trousers and at the same time closing the button on my shirt. After I had two sups of coffee and a drag on a cigarette, I was back on my toes rushing across town.

When I reached the Point, I sat down on a rock with the River Liffey behind me. A truck pulled over, the engine ticking. I heard a bell, its sound distant, but the rhythms clear. Everything was moving systematically, but all out of step with the man that was heading in my direction; his hair black, and greased back, his face fresh, eyes clear. He's a man the myth makers have a problem with because he is already a legend on our streets and the streets of Dublin. His name is Christy Dignam, his band Aslan. Christy had arranged for us to do an interview with him on RTE and also play a gig with his band. That's why I was waiting to see him.

The lorry pulled up and a man jumped out, complaining about

the tea he bought in the local shop. I turned away and glanced once again along the street as Christy came closer.

"Here, is that your man Christy Dignam out of Aslan?" he said, pointing to Christy. This was the man who penned the beautiful and powerful song 'This is'.

Christy called me from across the street avoiding the staring eyes of the man in the lorry. I rose off the rock, crossed the street, and followed him into the Point. Outside a small group of committed fans had already gathered. When we walked in the main act was on stage, the big English band, Tears for Fears.

The lead singer was playing the piano. He stood up and shook Christy's hand and nodded to me. I stood back, watching both bands go through the sound check. I had a few words with a boy called Alan, who had sat beside me in school all those years ago. It turned out he was Aslan's drummer.

After an hour or two passed, Christy jumped off the stage.

"What time are yah meeting Joe?"

"One o'clock," I replied.

"Right, me car is parked around the corner, come on I'll drop yah up."

I waved to the boys, wished them the best with the gig and left.

Christy had his glasses sitting on top of his head as we drove up through Sheriff Street. The car tore past the Custom House onto the Quays. He weaved in and out between the traffic. I sat white knuckled and glanced over my shoulder scanning the streets behind me, amazed at the distance we covered in such a short time.

"Don't believe everything they say about yah, or even half the stuff yah will read about yourselves in the future. Here what do yah think off this?" he said, opening up 'Hot Press' magazine, while keeping one hand on the steering wheel. In front of me was a page that was covered in photos of our band.

"Nice one," I said as we turned the corner, not so much because of his advice but for the vote of confidence that came with it.

"Your man, Corcoran, from RTE was onto me. He asked if Friday was alright for an interview," Christy said. "Is that ok with you and Joe?"

"Yeah! Absolutely."

"Yis aren't playing are yis?"

"Next Friday, I don't think so. I'll check with Joe."

"Nice one Christy," I said averting his gaze. I didn't want him to see how excited I was. I felt it was unprofessional.

When we arrived Joe was standing on the corner of Parnell Street. I was about ten minutes late. He looked worried because he knew when I said a time I was always there half an hour earlier.

Christy leaned over the dashboard, "Here Joe, I sorted the gig and the spot on RTE. George will put yah wide, I got to go."

"See yah later Christy,' we shouted as he waved and turned the car around.

"I thought you weren't coming," Joe said, looking a bit fed up.

"So did I, but I'm here now, come on."

We decided to take the Moore Street route. It is one of those heart-filled streets that always reminded me of the lower east side of New York from pictures I had seen.

"Get your ten bananas for fifty pence," the dealers shouted as we passed.

The sun was out and the streets were alive with people steeped in character. Some of these people came from our own neighbourhood, but most of them emerged from inner city dwellings.

Joseph and I were heading for a back lane that ran behind Henry Street. On the corner of one of the shops, smoke came from a copper pipe, it bellowed rising into the sky. The narrow streets had lines of makeshift stalls that accommodated mountains of fresh fruit and fresh fish.

"Yis look smashing," the old dealer said as we walked past,

dressed in large white caps, light shirts and braces.

"Thanks," we shouted back to the old Dublin lady who wore a dark blue apron over her clothes.

"Here, would yah not buy your poor oul mother a lovely bit of fish," she asked setting out the fish across a white board that sat on a silver cross pram.'

"Na you're alright missus."

"Ah go wan ou of tha, I'll give yah six pieces for two fifty. Here Mary, throw over a few of them bananas. Right, there's bananas an all for yis, yer mother'll be delira."

Joe looked at me and I looked at him, "Yah better buy something or we'll never get out of here," he said.

"Alright give us them" I said, as I handed her the money.

"I've no fifties, luv."

"It's alright, keep it," I said.

"Look, I'll catch yeh again."

Yah won't be catching me again, I thought to myself. But I had to admire her; she had done exactly what she had set out to do.

A man across the street brushed the dirt out of his shop as a group of fearless pigeons camped down along the shop fronts.

"Here twinny, catch," a neighbour shouted, as he threw two apples in our direction.

"Nice one," Joe shouted back after we caught them.

"Big hats or small heads," a voice roared. It was Dicko, a mate of mine who came from Summerhill. He was a fast talker and brilliant with the one liner.

He was standing next to a stall, his head held high and a cigarette hanging from his lip.

Dicko knew the streets, the dealers, the doormen and even the bouncers that hung on every nightclub door. He was a true inner city man who had a composure worth bottling. His hand was constantly in the air waving to passers-by.

"Who wants to buy the last of the apples, ten for fifty pence?"

were the words that rang above our heads. The sound of clogs clicking on the old cobble stones pinched my ear as the butcher across the street poured out a bucket of water.

"Where yis off to?" Dicko asked.

"Just down to a little record shop there behind Henry Street, to have a yap with a bloke."

"Yeah, what's the story?"

"Nothing much, just going to have a yap with this bloke about the single."

A tall lean man who wore black tight pants pranced by.

"Yis look lovely boys," he said, as he moved on. He walked like he was practising the foxtrot. He side-stepped an old women who was dressed in black and held a cross above her head, "Say a prayer for me," I heard Tight Pants shout back as he stopped and stared in a shop window paying homage to himself. I turned away as he went his way whistling.

"Yeah right, listen Dicko we better leg it; we have to meet this bloke in ten minutes," Joe said.

"Here before yis go. "Did yah here about the woman who shouted to her husband?"

"No" we said in unison, hoping this joke would be a short one.

"She said, 'Johnny I'd luv to do something different'. Johnny paused for a moment and shouted back: 'Right, Mary, try making me dinner'."

We laughed mostly with relief because the joke was a short one. We shook hands and left our inner-city friend, before he broke into his next set of jokes

"Catch yah later," we shouted as we made a fast dive for Henry Street. I dropped the bag of fish into the hands of a small woman who had a gang of kids hanging out of her. Her eyes opened wide as if she had a Damascus experience.

"Ah thanks very much luv," she cried, as I walked on.

Joe and I stood on the corner under a street lamp while we

waited for the van to arrive; I lit up a cigarette, and watched carefully. We were like captains, awaiting the arrival of the foot-soldiers.

Just then our army descended onto the streets, nodding as they passed us. We watched them going in and out of the record shops. Other men collected the bags of records. They were dropped at their feet, as the droppers moved on.

"There he is," Joe whispered as we spotted the van pull up in the back lane. The back door opened and boxes were pushed in. The others filled the van with bags and then went back to their station. The shopkeeper walked out, gave us a slight nod while the van driver waved and moved onto the next shop. The army walked across the bridge that was called after a coin.

"Right Joe, I got to go and try me wedding suit on," I said.

"I'll go with yah."

♪

Sandra and I had made a date. It was 27 June 1990. I looked in the mirror dressed in the black wedding suit. There was a small speaker over my head. The radio played the charts. "Now, straight in at number twenty-one - 'I Surrender' by the D11-Runners." I pulled the light curtain back and both of us spoke simultaneously, "We did it...WE DID IT."

When I had finished dealing with the tailor and all the suits were packed, we left the shop and hurried up the street. Time was rushing past. I had to meet Sandra, her parents and her cousin James at her mother's house. But I wasn't to arrive alone, my suitcase was to come with me because this was the evening that all our belongings including the five tier cake were to travel to the hotel.

I dropped the case in the hall and raced up the stairs. Sandra was sitting at the dressing table putting the finishing touches to her make up. She smiled, it was an encouraging smile that told me she had heard the news about the single.

"If you would permit me, I would like to ask for your hand in marriage," I said jokingly.

"Ok. I'll marry you tomorrow at two, don't forget to bring a suit,"she replied.

The door of her bedroom was opened, I could see her parents chatting to James.

"Right Sandra, let's go," I said.

She rose off the chair, looked in the mirror and followed me down the stairs.

The drive to the hotel was about forty minutes. I gazed out the window as we sped down the long narrow country roads.

"Here George," Sandra's father said. "You're some tulip; yah must be fond of wedding cake."

"I am Harry."

"I gave me wedding dress away," he joked, while eyeing Sandra's mother who was busy talking to James.

"I was going to be a nun but they said there was none wanted, so I became daddy bear instead. That's mammy bear and that's one of the baby bears," he said lightly tipping Sandra in the ribs. "Here James! Are you still doing the cooking up in that place?"

"Yeah, I'm still there Harry."

"Do yah do a nice steak up there?"

"Ah, I only do the best Harry."

"The last time George had steak he bit his tongue."

"I think I'd be better off sticking to fish Harry, don't you?" I said pointing to my mid section.

"Go way out of that, sure there's more meat on a herring-bone."

"This is it now," James cut in, as he pulled into the large car park.

When we went inside Sandra's parents slipped away to make sure everything was in order while we sat in the large conservatory talking with James. When they arrived back at the table they were accompanied by another couple about their own age. So we sat and talked about the usual jokes that were told before a couple got married.

Sandra got up and walked towards the ladies room. When she came out I was standing behind a pillar. "Sandra," I called in a whisper. She turned, I caught her hand and we ran, sneaking outside.

We sat on a little stone wall that had leaves growing out of it and we watched the sun say goodbye to the day. The moon made a flamboyant appearance, throwing sharp straps of light at the lilacs, under the tree. But I cast my eye upon a more beautiful sight that was sitting beside me, in her short mini and long brown legs. Then we stared dreamily across the countryside. She rested her head upon my shoulder, remaining silent.

The hollow voice of the wind rushed around. This was the night before all nights, the day before the morning, a morning that will run into the day, as the day runs into a lifetime.

An old man, who wore long whiskers and smoked a pipe walked past.

"It's a fine evening," he said.

"That it is, sir, that it is," I replied.

I took her in my arms, held her tightly and whispered, "Let love fill your heart and don't be captured by anything that would stain your kind nature. Now, shake the hand that shook the world, the hand of George Fitzgerald." With those words she broke into a fit of laughter, I felt it rise from her stomach.

"You're a philosopher full and gifted, in the art of dramatics," she said, breaking out into laughter again.

"That I am my dear, that I am. Now let's go," I said taking her hand.

"Where?"

"To the future my dear, to the future."

♪

The sky couldn't have been any brighter on our special day. The golden radiance shone down on us as if God himself had come out to mark the day with a smile. When we walked down the long marble steps in front of the altar, we walked down as Husband and wife.

As we left the church, a gentle wind as smooth as velvet wrapped itself around us as the crowd in front cheered and our family and friends clapped in joyful celebration.

"We did it," I whispered, squeezing her hand.

"We did," she replied, her long black hair flowing down onto her shoulder.

Her white dress was the finest I'd ever seen. The music from the church could still be heard. I rubbed my hand over my shaven head as I cast my eyes across the church and caught sight of Toma. He stood among the crowd remaining in silent appraisal.

I turned away and stared at the sun, my mind became occupied, busy. Then I broke away from the handshakes, kisses and hugs and met him at the side of the church. The very place we played as boys. Toma reached out his hand, our pulses ran together.

"Yah did it, Georgie."

"With the help of God, Toma."

I tugged him.

"Here, what's your name?" He smiled back and followed me.

"Thomas."

"I'm George. That's my twin brother and the other fella is Pat."

We burst out laughing and in the middle of the laughter I said to him, from now on, you'll be known as Toma."

"Yeah and you'll be known as Twinny."

We embraced in a tight hug that was engrafted into a larger hug that came from Joe, Pat, Weller, and Paulo and even little

Wesley.

Then the chauffeur stepped out, opened the back door of the Rolls-Royce. Sandra took my hand and we ran under the hail of flowers that fell from heaven. I stood at the door with my arm stretched out and caught a white flower, its petals springing up into the afternoon sky. I waved and jumped into the car. We sped off with the large black limousine following.

The car followed the road and street that I ran on when I was a kid. Then it passed the school where we first met. I looked out the window and caught sight of a man I knew carrying a paper under his arm. It was Harry my friend. In my hand was a small white ball on a stalk, the reminder of the flower I'd caught earlier. His words came to mind, the ones he had spoken all those years ago. "Become a pearl."

I glanced up towards the rear-view mirror and saw him wave. I caught the smile on his face and smiling I muttered, "Thanks Harry, thanks."

His words stayed with me as we travelled along the narrow country road, towards the hotel. When the car pulled over, I noticed a young boy and girl standing at the pillars.

"Here," I said as I walked over to the boy handing him the white ball, saying: "To catch a pearl become a pearl!" They looked at me with a bewildered look on their faces.

"You don't look like a pearl," the young boy shouted as I walked away.

"That's because you're looking at the shell, the pearl is inside."

"I'll remember that," he shouted, looking into his girlfriend's eyes.

There were about two hundred people there at the end of the night. A great university of working class passion filled the large reception area. The dance floor cleared when Sandra and I stepped forward and danced under a glitterball, our first dance as a married couple.

"You like to dance," she whispered.

"Only in the company of another dancer," I replied.

After the reception Sandra and I stood in the centre of the large dance floor while everyone circled around. They all proposed a toast, embracing us and wishing us well.Then they crossed their arms with each other and we went under and out the door into the waiting taxi that escorted us to a more private hotel.

The next day we headed to Portugal for three weeks with two of our friends.

It was while we sat at the pool in the hot sun that we got a phone call that informed us that one of our band members, Ken Mc Cluskey, was auditioning for a part in the Alan Parker film, 'The Commitments'.

The three weeks were swallowed up in fun, laughter, and the most pleasurable holiday I had experienced.

A few days after we got back we all auditioned for the 'The Commitments.' Ken our guitarist had gotten a leading part. One by one we were called in to read the script in front of the legendary director Alan Parker. Jackie got a small role while the rest of us were picked to play extras. Louis Walsh was now our agent. It was while we were on the set of the film that Peter told us he was meeting Louis a few blocks up the Quay. So Joe and I took the walk up and met him.

Louis was sitting facing us when we walked in. The first thing I noticed about Louis was his youthful looks. We had heard that this guy was around the music game a long time. So I was expecting to see an old bald-headed man dressed in a cheap suit wearing even cheaper jewellery. But, surprisingly, he didn't look much older than us.

The second thing I noticed was his reassuring smile that helped us relax. Little did he know then that he was only one band away from the big time and international stardom. Peter was to his right. Two members of the Hot House Flowers were sitting behind while Rob Strong was at the bar. Louis didn't pull punches. He started off the meeting by telling us that there was a gig coming up, it was to be staged in the park, and it was going to be the largest lark in the park in the history of the state.

"What's the chance of us getting the gig?" Joe asked. He didn't pull punches either.

"Yeah need another hit single. And soon."

"We're working hard, Louis. We're going straight to Windmill to record after the film."

"Well the good news is, I have the band booked to open a festival in Galway next week with Brian Kennedy," Peter said. We were still sitting at the table when Maria Doyle Kennedy came in. Maria was sound and a great singer and actress. She came straight over and began chatting with us. There was a brilliant buzz around, everyone was doing well, it was a great time to be in a band in Dublin.

Maria moved on and so did we. We finished on the set and recorded our single. It was called 'Yeah Yeah,' and distributed by EMI. We did the gig in Galway and the single reached number thirteen in the charts, our second 'hit' single.

The large mass of black clouds that had gathered in the sky finally erupted. I stood at the window and turned towards the video that was playing.

"Is that any good Sandra?"

"Yeah,"she said as she lay slumped across the chair.

"Is it nearly over?"

She nodded.

"When yah say nearly over, does that mean one minute or ten?"

She narrowed her eyes and pressed her head into the cushion. "Well."

"Well what?"

"Is it nearly over?"

"Yeah, yeah. What's the rush?"

"Great, cause I've got a video I want to watch."

"What's it about?"

"It's about a bloke growing up in New York, he meets a girl and gets married and stuff."

"What stuff?"

"Well his name is Joe Valachi, he was the first man to openly speak about the Mafia."

"Oh no, not another gangster movie?" she said as she sat up on the chair.

"Na it's not really a gangster film, he gets married an all, I told yah."

So we had a romantic night in, in the presence of Lucky Luciano, Vinto Genovese and not forgetting Joseph Valachi.

The phone rang and I answered it in my best New York accent.

"That was Joe - he's up in me ma's house. I think I'll go up to the house 'cause Sheba needs a walk."

Sheba was a Staffordshire. We only had her a week or so, but already we were growing very fond of her.

"Here I'll grab a curry and drop the video back."

"Ok see yah later."

"Right, come on Sheba," I shouted grabbing her lead.

As I walked towards the end of the lane, I saw two men standing under a street light, one was long-limbed and boney, and the other one had a large scar across his face. I kept walking, Sheba was pushing forward breathing heavily.

The gentlemen separated, and the long fella, known as Benny, walked under a canopy of a nearby house and slid down the side entrance.

I stopped at the end of the lane and lit up a smoke. The rain was getting heavier, Sheba was growling. I switched my glance towards the other man who went by the name of Paddy The Lip. I looked back and saw another boney figure staring at me from the shadows of the lane.

Sheba began to bark; I ruffled the top of her head whispering, "There's a good girl."

The door of a house opened. Benny walked out. A mobile rang; Paddy answered it. He began to roar and scream. I saw a young boy groping his way along the streets shouting: "Benny, yah ripped me off. Yah ripped me off!"

Benny growled at him and pulled him by the jaw. Then he slapped him until he fell to the ground. He walked proudly towards Paddy, fixing the collars of his jacket. When he reached him I saw him hand him some money

I heard my name being called, through a voice that was barely audible. I grabbed hold of the lead, and stared at the figure that was moving towards me. His head was covered by a hoody and a long coat was draped over him like a blanket.

The heavens opened and the thunder roared. A chill ran through me, I felt it cling to my bones. My name was mentioned again. The hooded man was now within handshaking distance. He stood under a street light. It revealed his face. And I muttered, "Sonny!"

He was thin, his eyes were sunk, and he coughed heavily. "Gis a smoke will, yah George?" he asked when the coughing stopped.

Anto crawled up behind him; he didn't look too good either. I looked at Sonny in disbelief and remembered the little boy I had grown up with. And the words the woman once said sprang to mind: "That boy will die young."

"Ah there yah are, Sonny me oul mate. Come're," Paddy The Lip called.

Sonny and Anto scurried over. He gave them something, like the kind gentleman he was. They ran back down the lanes, shaking, trembling, slipping, and sliding upon the bricks and rubble. When they got to the end of the lane, Sonny stopped and grimaced as the wind and the rain swished against his face. I caught his stare and then remembered his word, "Did yah think I would leave yah there?"

A skinny kid with bright hair called to me:

"Give us a smoke, Twin."

It was the kid that Benny had beaten. He walked over to me, wearing no jacket, soaked to the skin.

"The gear has us Twin, it has us."

I felt a deep sense of shock and pity when I looked at him; it paralysed me.

He drew near, I touched his shoulder. He gripped my hand tearfully.

"It has me. It has me, Twin."

"I know," I replied as I pulled him close.

"Sorry Twin."

"Here, don't be worrying," I said, reaching into my pocket, giving him the packet of smokes. "Listen to what a man once told me- he said that someone up there likes me. Yah know what I believe?"

"What's that Twin?"

"That he likes you too."

"God an' all Twin?"

"Yeah, Jesus yah know what I mean?"

"I hope he looks after me ma, her poor heart is broke. Nice one, Twin," he shouted running down the lane, towards the others.

The next time I saw him, his picture appeared in the evening newspaper. He was stabbed to death, at the age of eighteen.

I watched Paddy The Lip, as he drove by laughing. He stopped the car and called his gentleman friend.

"Are yah right, Benny, we've dazzled them enough." The words he had shared with Sonny rushed across my mind:

"Tell 'em that drugs are great. Give them it for nothing. Fill their minds with the thought of how great the high is and when they're caught, they'll be ours for life."

"Here which one's the bull dog?" Benny said as he ran for the car.

"Go on Sheba," I shouted, letting her off the lead.

But he made it into the car and sped off staring out at me.

I headed towards the curry shop and met little Bo. He was a kid that lived a few blocks from me. I could see by his eyes that he was caught too.

After I reported the story to Sandra, I kneeled and prayed. "*Dear Lord Jesus help us. I don't want to leave Sonny there, but I can't help him. But your word says who ever asks he does receive so I ask you, to help him please Amen. And don't forget little Bo.*"

When I got up the next morning I washed, dressed, and brought Sandra her breakfast.

"What time is it?"

"Ten passed ten," Sandra said as I cleared the table.

"Right, I'd better phone Joe."

I put the call in and Joe answered.

"What time have we to be there?"

"Twelve o' clock at the studio."

"Right see yah there," I replied and put down the phone.

When we got to the studio I crossed the floor and sat down, watching Joe and Weller walking up and down talking on phones.

I felt Sandra's gaze on me.

"Are yah all right?"

I shook my head.

"Are yah sure?" she asked.

"Yeah, just a bit nervous before the gig."

Everyone was talking about us; we had just finished a tour in which we played the National Concert Hall, the Olympia and the Point Depot in conjunction with the Alan Parker Film. Some of the band had been interviewed on RTE's 'Dempsey's Den' and on the 'Beat Box' by Simon Young.

We were now grossing £1,500 a gig. A few nights before we played one song in front of a star-studded crowd and received £10,000! And afterwards we drank with the Rolling Stones, Alan Parker, film stars, and top models.

We also played a gig in Limerick where there was so many people the bouncers had to make two single lines to get us from the dressing room to the stage. After the gig the door of the dressing-room was kicked in by adoring fans, screaming for autographs.

The next day we were invited to a special showing of the film. As the film closed the audience gave us a standing ovation and it must have taken us a half an hour to get back into the hired cars.

Eddie Rowley had run a story in the popular 'Sunday World' with the headline: *Runners Have The World at their Feet*. And we felt we had the world at our feet because we were about to play in the biggest Lark in the Park in the history of the state.

There was a knock on the door. Jackie opened it. Ken O' Brien walked in, he was one of our roadies and chiefly responsible for all the organisation for the day.

"There's an English bloke downstairs. He's looking for yis. Will I tell him to come up?"

"Where's Peter," Jackie asked.

"He's gone ahead with Jerry to make sure everything is set up," Ken replied.

Before Ken could say anything more, there was another knock on the door.

"Is this where the D11 Runners are?" an English voice asked.

"He kept his word," Joe said as he put the phone down.

The man was a reporter for an English paper. A photographer came in behind him and started taking photographs. The phones were ringing. The English man put down his tape recorder, all eyes were on him. He smiled, gave a little sigh and he said, "By the way the BBC have picked up on your singles," and then pressed the button down.

We did the interview and the story broke in the English papers a week later.

"Right boys and girls, it time to go. There's 70,000 people waiting on yis," Kenny said.

When we drove into the Phoenix Park, we couldn't believe our eyes. There were barriers everywhere, roadies, reporters, band member's, managers, PR people and a stage of the likes only seen in Live Aid.

When it was our time to go on, we climbed the stage one by one. Joe walked out in front with his hand straight out. Paulo started with a drum beat, Pat followed on percussions. The band waited and Paulo shouted, "One, two, three, four...", and we burst into the set with the largest crowd of people we ever saw chanting our name. Joe ran to one side, Pat to the other while I slid in between them, with 70,000 people cheering us on.

Our videos were starting to be aired on TV in Europe and the US, while radio shows, the posters, the stories in the papers also added to the hype. The money, the hit singles...they were all great. But this moment only happens in dream world, and we were living it.

The crowd was beginning to get stirred up, from one end of the park to the other, armed with shouts and cries until it sounded like the roaring of the sea. Then one by one we exited the stage until the only one left was Paulo playing the drums. He stopped and we listened to our name being lifted up to heaven. When the gig finished we were whisked away. We showered, dressed up and were escorted to a local pub. We were given champagne while every eye was on us. The DJ announced our presence and played our two hit singles. Tony St Ledger met us for a drink. He counselled us to remain steadfast in learning our art. "Keep your head on the ground and your eyes fixed on your music." Then he said, "I think yis are going to make it."

After the gig in the Park, doors began to fly open. Everything improved, from the clothes we wore, to the transport we used, even the dressing rooms we used. It seemed that our name was on everyone's lips from the cats and dogs in the alley to the record producers, even 'Hot Press' took note.

Joe received a phone call from Louis. He told him he had set up an interview with the rock journalist Damian Corless. Joe did the interview and the full page article appeared in the following issue of 'Hot Press'. Simon Young was constantly playing the bands video, on his weekly show, 'The Beat Box'. Tony Fenton was pushing the single along his hit list, this was our cue to go in and record our next single, "People Lets Dance". It went to number ten in the charts.

Rizzo looked anxiously around as he stood on the corner of Abbey Street. I shuffled towards him with the collar of my jacket pulled up and my hands buried deep in my pockets.

"Here, did yah hear the news? Number ten."

He switched his glance and gave me a sour smile. He doesn't-look too happy, I thought. I shook his hand. He stared at his boots, then we broke away.

"Is everything alright?" I asked.

He looked uncomfortable

"Yeah, Yeah."

Somehow I didn't believe him.

"So, what's happenin'?" I asked loudly.

"What de yah mean?" he paused; I said nothing.

"Oh the single, yeah great, number ten. Yis'll be number one next week," he replied, winking.

"That's right. I'm meeting Joe and Weller, they've gone to get the figures."

Although I was looking directly at him, I felt he was staring through me.

"Here, are yah alright?" I asked again.

"Yeah listen, I need to go somewhere. Tell Joe, I'll ring him."

"Yeah ok. Nice one."

It was Thursday morning, that was the morning all the figures came in. And it was also the morning we would hear if the single had gone up or down in the charts.

"Right, Joe, what did yah hear?" He and Weller looked excited.

"Number One, can yah believe it."

"What! Are yah serious?"

We grabbed each others hand, "Number one," we all shouted as we burst out laughing

"What did they say, what did they say?"

"They said we did enough singles, not only to go to number one, but to stay there next week as well."

I couldn't believe it. We were the band with two hit singles and now we had a number one. And the best news for us was that we knew we weren't doing it alone. There is no way you can go to the number one spot from buying a few hundred singles from a few small shops in Dublin. Anyway when our spotters went into buy the singles from HMV and Virgin, they were already sold out. Outside the city we found the same thing had happened. The number one spot was without a doubt out ticket to the big time.

That Sunday Joe, Pat, Jackie, Sandra, and I sat listening to the music charts in my ma's house. Nervously, I was stuck to the chair with my hands between my legs and my eyes staring to the ground.

"Did they say it yet?" ma asked.

"No, not yet, Ma," the three of us quickly replied.

"Higher it up; I can't hear it," da said.

"*And now, this weeks number one...*"

We all looked at each other and then he mentioned some other band. I was so shocked I can't remember who it was. Silence filled the room; the room yah wouldn't swing a cat in...the room where I nearly burst the glass-fitting when we had our first jamming session.

"Are yah sure yis were number one?" ma asked.

"Ma, we got the figures, the bloke told us that we sold enough to stay at number one for at least a week," Joe said.

I flew into a rage; Joe started punching the chair.

"Give it up boys," da said. "It's disgraceful, yah can't go from number one to nowhere, I'm telling yah, Marie."

"Ma, we sent gangs into buy the single all over the place. It was sold out," Pat said. The phone was hopping. I nodded for Joe to follow me upstairs.

"It's Rizzo, I know it's him," I said, with my eyes red and my teeth grinding.

"How de yah know?"

"I met that sleveen, remember. I knew something was up the way he was talking."

We punched the air, kicked the bed, and sat down gutted. It was Sunday, there was nothing we could do but sit it out.

The next morning, Joe Paulo and I rushed across town to Peter's office. Peter glanced up from behind his desk when we came charging in the door.

"What's going on Peter? It was him, Rizzo wasn't it?" I said, the tone of my voice was angry. Joe was strangely calm, Paulo said nothing. Peter motioned with his hands for us to close the door.

"Look, Louis was on to me. As far as he can gather hundreds of singles have gone missing."

Peter again motioned with his hands for us to sit down while picking up the phone. "Right Dave you be in the studio around six o' clock the boys will meet yah there ok." He put the phone down.

"Yis are going in to record a cover something that people can quickly identify with. Dave Brown the guitarist out of 'Little Sister Sage' is going to help rush it together. We're also bringing in session workers to fill out the brass. Tony St Ledger was on to me, he's going to co-ordinate everything."

"What cover are we doing" Paulo asked?

"The Stones. 'Satisfaction'."

When we got home, I walked around the house talking to myself then I came up with an idea. "I'll go to see Shay."

The afternoon sky was faultless bright blue with a crimson ribbon hovering in the distant horizon. I jumped off the bike and stood under a large tree to shade myself from the sun. I lit up a smoke, and stared into the plot of vegetables that occupied Decourcie Square.

Anticipation was a word I could use to describe the feelings I was experiencing as I looked forward to meeting Shay. When I turned the corner my feelings of anticipation were instantly dashed. I took the last drag on my cigarette and flicked it away. The old cobble shop was no longer there. A house stood in its place.

My mind drifted again, I saw the bright sparkling days, and the dark winter nights, I listened to the hissing sound of the burnt kettle. I saw the little boys in the caps eating ice cream while the old man sat on a stuffed chair. I remembered his words. "Georgie son, one day you're going to be a great man you'll reach great heights."

"Will I?"

"Yes, no doubt."

"Will yah be there Shay?"

I recalled the look he had on his face.

"Georgie son, close your eyes."

I did. "Can yah see me?"

"I can, Shay."

"I'll be there."

A young woman passed me dressed in fine clothes. She turned her head towards me. I caught her gaze and averted her stare.

"Can I help you?" she asked in a gentle voice.

"No thanks. I was looking for an old teacher friend, who used to work here, but I'm afraid he's moved."

"I wasn't aware that a teacher lived in these streets," she replied her voice sounding puzzled.

"Oh yeah, there was a man that lived and worked in these streets who was one of the best teachers I ever had, but he's no longer here, he's moved."

"Ah, that's sad," she replied softly. "Do you know where he is gone?"

"Yes, I replied he's just gone over the wall."

I jumped on my bike and cycled off. I looked back to where the old cobbler shop once stood. In my mind's eye I could see Shay dressed in his apron, waving, while the little boys in their caps and braces danced and laughed in the old cobble streets. I turned my head quickly holding back the tears and muttered,

"Goodbye Shay, goodbye my dear old friend."

When I got home Joe was at my house.

"Joe yah know what? Shay's dead."

"Poor oul Shay," he replied. There was a minute silence. And then he spoke,

"Did yah hear the news?"

"No, what news?"

"Rizzo's stuck his head up and offered us £10,000 to record an album."

"What, how come?"

"I don't know. Somethings not right. We get pulled at number ten and he comes along and offers us £10,000."

"Do yah want my opinion?" I said.

"Yeah."

"We're being ripped."

"Yeah, Rizzo moved too quickly. The question is - what's behind it?"

"I'll phone Louis in the morning," Joe said, pulling himself up off the chair.

Louis Walsh, found out that the money wasn't coming from Rizzo at all, in fact it was coming from EMI France, and it was closer to £100,000.

The good news was that EMI France was showing great interest in signing the band. A company called BMG was also interested. And there was another eight companies behind them. Up until now, our singles had been distributed by EMI Ireland, but we switched to Sony.

We went on tour shortly after in which we played with The Specials, The Beat, and The Cranberries, making a special appearance with Rob Strong.

But there was a major problem. EMI France wanted the sole rights of the singles we'd released. The problem was the three singles were tied to Rizzo's company and we needed him to release them in order to move on. But he wasn't that kind. So in a desperate bid to solve the problem, our manager followed that company to a music convention in the US.

A reporter from 'The European' newspaper was in a hotel interviewing the band, a week after our manager had left for the States. A phone call came in the middle of the interview informing us that the Rizzo refused to accept the deal that our manager offered. His trip to the U.S was a complete waste of time.

I took a deep breath and tried to control my anger. I handed the phone back to Joe, who was equally red-faced. It was quickly arranged that we meet Peter the following week as soon as he arrived home.

♪

Weller, Joe and I raced across the street and grabbed a taxi. Weller was whispering in Joe's ear. I was sitting in the front. We were all very tense. The meeting was to take place in a car park in the inner city. So this brought a question mark to our minds. It really indicated that this was going to be a rushed meeting.

The car turned into the large open spaces. The taxi man took the money but glanced at us very suspiciously.

Peter was standing at his car, leaning against the door. He was dressed in a long mac and a very expensive two piece dark navy suit. We moved across the car park between cars. Joe and I dressed in caps and long coats. Weller had his hair in a pony with the sides shaved.

Peter smiled and shook our hands individually. He had the contracts that came from EMI. After a few words we got into the car. I opened the window, the night air was crisp.

Peter began to talk. I stared at him with deep scepticism, wondering who was making the real blunder here.

"So what's the deal?" Joe asked his voice was slightly aggressive.

"Well there's no deal, if Rizzo doesn't co-operate."

There was a long pause.

"But I believe we can work that out," he then said.

He sounded like he was really trying to convince himself. His words fell on deaf ears because we were not convinced.

After I advertised this, a small controlled argument broke out. I jumped out of the car, slammed the door and walked away. I glanced back to Peter. He flashed me a smile. It was forced, but he made the effort. When I walked back to the car, he tried to reassure us that he would do his best. He was a man of his word and he had our best interest at heart.

We stepped out of the car and walked back towards the city. There was one thing on our minds. It was without a doubt make or break time and we knew it full well.

♪

Right in the centre of all the running around in the jet propelling life of the music game, the phone rang. Behind the phone call was a dream about to be fulfilled. It informed us that we were booked to make an appearances on 'The Late, Late Show'.

We were all sitting in the dressing room waiting to go on stage, when the room was suddenly filled with excitement. Not because we were booked for another TV appearance, but because of the viewing power of 'The Late, Late, Show'. It was our chance to be exposed to the nation. We decided that, well maybe it was decided for us that we'd play our latest single- 'Satisfaction'. We hired some new session workers to fill out the brass section, just to give it more body. By this time we had become very familiar with the RTE studios - the dressing rooms and the narrow corridors behind the scenes.

Joe Duffy had played a major role in all of this and we were grateful. He had been plugging the band behind the curtain of the entertainment business for a long time. He is a good man of strong character, on fire with a vision for a new Dublin. We admired this and respected him.

Gay Byrne was indeed a very pleasant man. Although he is very powerful he has a very gentle way about him. When he introduced the band, he mentioned that Joe Duffy was plugging us from behind the scenes. We did the show and went down quite well.

♪

Sandra and I had received the best news ever. We were expecting, or at least Sandra was. We were very excited and although it was early days, we were already making plans. Sandra would be looking in all the baby shops, thinking what she would buy when the baby was born.

The weeks flew by and at three and a half months, Sandra got the chicken pox. She went to the hospital and everything seemed fine. She wasn't booked to have a scan until four weeks later.

Joe summoned us for a meeting. We met in a little village type restaurant across town. He told us from the outset that the single had been pulled and that there wasn't much hope for our latest single. In short, we had grown too powerful on our own. And certain people out there didn't like it. So we were whacked. And that's that.

The stations stopped playing our singles, doors began to close in our faces, and there was nothing our manager could do. As the meeting was coming to a close. Joe informed us that lurking in the background was a powerful manager who had approached him. But Joe turned him down.

I was dreaming about kids and fatherhood and secretly I thought that if the worst came to the worst after the baby was born Sandra could go back to modelling. She was now twenty weeks into the pregnancy.

"Right, let's leg it," Joe said and we promptly sped home.

When I walked into the house I sensed something was wrong. Sandra wasn't home. Before I reached the kitchen the phone rang, I answered it.

"Hello, are you Mr Fitzgerald?" The voice sounded very officious.

"Yeah that's right."

"You're needed in the hospital straight away; your wife needs to see you."

"Is the baby ok?" But somehow I knew that the answer was going to be no.

"Well I can't really discuss that over the phone, I would rather speak to you in person."

"Well I want to know as you are speaking to me, is my baby ok." She paused for a moment and said, "I am sorry."

My heart began to beat faster. A wave of shock overcame me. "Mr Fitzgerald, Mr Fitzgerald," the nurse kept calling.

I stood there in a hell-filled silence and put down the phone.

The smell of chaos filled my nostrils as I entered the ward. There were rows of beds filled with expectant mothers. To the left of the doorway a curtain was drawn. I pulled it back. Sandra was laying sideways on the bed. She turned quickly. I met her pain-filled stare.

"We've lost the baby," I sighed

She closed her eyes. I felt as if the ground was opening up and I was being swallowed alive. Sandra turned away, biting hard down on her knuckle. I stared at her without speaking. She turned her face toward me. I swallowed hard. The light was dull, a small harsh man was standing at the bedside reading a chart. When he left I met her stare again. "One in heaven," I said quietly. There was a long silence. She turned rubbing her hand against her face trying hard to block out the world. I stared at the ground. She handed me a tiny baby grow - one she had bought that day. I felt helpless. I heard laughter in the distance, women congratulating each other. I just wanted to run.

"I'll see yah later," I said as I walked out. I could hear her crying as the door closed behind me.

On the way out, I went by a ward full of mothers and their babies. Christmas decorations hung from the walls and the nurses were decorating a small tree. Everyone seemed to be smiling, but I couldn't enter into the festive spirit. I stood in a corner. It was dark. I pressed my hands against my eyes because I wanted the world to go away. I didn't know it then and maybe it was as well, twelve months later, on Christmas week, the same thing happened again.

On the way home the wind and the rain blew hard against me. The clouds were dark. A thundering sound roared across the night sky and large drops of rain fell. Across the street a man was shouting as he stood at his makeshift stall selling newspapers.

It was only a five minute walk to the bus stop but I kept my head down clutching at any wall or the shelter of a doorway that had an open space.

I visited a friend's grave. The fallen leaves made a rustling sound as they blew around my feet. I stood in silence; his age came into focus only, twenty two years.

"Say hello to our baby for us Lord," I requested, then left and headed home to the empty house.

A few days after Sandra got out of hospital, Joe came up to see us. He tied his little Staffordshire terrier to a pole outside the house and came in full of chat.

I wasn't very talkative. Sandra was upstairs lying down.

Joe stood up and walked across the floor. He stood by the fire, falling immediately in to his natural role as a brother, trying as best as he could to put me at ease while I stared into space.

The sound of the heavy traffic outside caught my attention. I noticed a caravan of people coming up the passage. I pressed my face in my hands which signalled a steady release of breath. I didn't feel very sociable Joe answered the door. After a few words, everything went quiet again. I reached up and pulled the curtain. Sandra must be up, I thought, as I could smell dinner being cooked. She brought Joe in some dinner. I wasn't hungry, but she insisted I eat something. I remember that dinner - potatoes, steak and beans. I felt a wave of compassion fill me, but I hadn't the words to express it. There she was, our baby dead, and yet still serving.

"Thanks Sandra," we both said.

"Are you not having anything?" I asked.

"Yeah, I'll have some later," she replied quietly.

"Here Joe, I promise yah this - If I get through this, I'll never be the same again. It's taken something out of me.' And we're out of the band, that's it for us," I said.

"Never promise anything, especially when it comes to the future."

"What do yah mean?"

Our conversation changed course and my thoughts escorted me into another realm. I walked across the dormitory of a childless marriage, every door empty, no little feet in these rooms. I sat back, placed the empty plate on the floor, and stared blankly into the fire. There was a knock on the door. It was da, and ma, and Wesley. Joe answered it. I placed a mask on, hiding my true emotions. I didn't want to worry them. I forced a smile and tried to be brave.

When everyone was gone I walked into the kitchen. Sandra had gone to bed.

I walked upstairs and looked in at her. She had drifted to sleep. The light was on in the bathroom. I slipped across the floor quietly to switch it off. I was afraid to wake her. At least in sleep, there was peace. In that world she could play with her children and laugh, running through the meadows. I closed the door, placed my hands on my face and rubbed hard against my skin.

My body began to shake. I pressed my head against the wall, clenched my fist, pushing hard against the concrete. I fell to my knees. Anger blinded me. Rage consumed me; loneliness clothed me like a garment. Mental weight was my companion. But there was something inside bubbling. It was soft, quick and gentle. Words of compassion that said: "Let the little children come to me, for theirs is the Kingdom of God."

Like I said, the following Christmas we lost another baby. I can remember running across The Ha'penny Bridge, listening to a mocking voice in my head saying, where's your God now? I stopped, looked towards the sky and said, "The Lord gives, and the Lord takes away. Blessed be the name of the Lord."

It was around this time that I became great friends with a man called Peter Traynor. I had met Peter while working on a project in the inner city around 1990. He was without doubt, the most important man that ever crossed my path. A man of great learning gifted in the word of God. He encouraged me to read and he prayed for me constantly. By this time the band was finished. I was out of work so I took to the drink a bit. I asked God for help and then read, 'See there was a man sent from God' and I thought.

"Peter."

"Will the Lord give us a child, Peter? I asked over a coffee one morning.

"George, the best is yet to come."

I told him about Sonny, Bo and Anto. He opened up the word, read, prayed, and I believed.

On the 18th of December 1994, I walked into a ward in the same hospital. Sandra was lying down, her hands were straight out, and they were full. A baby was smiling up at her.

"Look there's your Daddy," she said as she handed him to me.

"Yah done good Sandra, yah done well," I said, as I lifted him high and muttered, "You shall be raised in riches, for I can see a prince in you, son."

"What will we call him?" she asked.

"Well, we've been sitting in a den of lions, waiting for this fella to arrive. So he shall be called Daniel, the Lord has given us a gift, so his full name shall be Daniel Jonathan Fitzgerald."

The following day, as I was on my way up to the hospital, I noticed the big brown dog sitting in the shop window. I had seen him so many times before as I walked past everyday, I always told myself, someday I'll buy that for my baby. And would you believe it, there he was. It was as if he had been waiting for me. I went into the shop. There wasn't very much room in the little shop on account of it being Christmas. Throngs of people were in every doorway, scooping up all the latest bargains. I went straight up to the counter

"Could I have that dog please?"I blurted a bit impatiently while pointing to it, hoping no one else would get there before me.

"Certainly sir," the elderly lady said.

I didn't even ask how much it cost.

"Just hang on a minute and I'll get you a fresh one."

"No, I want that one on display."

"Oh, are you sure?" she said, looking a bit puzzled.

"I can't give you any discount."

"I don't want any discount, this is the one I want," I said clutching it, under my arm. She stared at me for a moment and then smiled. I picked up a lovely card. On the front was the words - *Happy Christmas Son*. Soft music could be heard in the background. I looked again at the card and muttered under my breath, "Happy Christmas son. Thank you Lord, thank you." A tiny tear slid down my cheek. I wiped it quickly with the back of my hand, handed the lady the money and walked out.

It was a very cold day but I didn't care. When I arrived at the hospital Sandra was sitting under a large tree that was set beside the window. A winter sun suddenly turned up and it shone through the glass. I stood and stared at her for a moment as she rocked the bundle of joy in her arms.

"Right let's bring this little fella home," I said as I helped her to her feet.

♪

I was working in the kitchens of an old Dublin Hotel at this time. It came through a friend of mine who's name was Mick. When I arrived home, Mick phoned and told me that when I started back I was going to be working in the 'cellar' with him. That was great news at the time.

Mick smiled at me so I smiled back. He was a man of very strong muscular build. His shoulders were square and his waist was narrow. Light sandy colour hair graced his head that was cut tight. And he wore a Borstal spot on the side of his cheek. He was a great man to be around. There was something very special about him, but I don't think he knew that.

The heavy dark green door made a creaking sound as he turned the long key. The door opened and we walked into the cellar. Along the wall there were six arched cells that had bars in the front, with silver gates in the centre. The white-washed walls had paint that was peeling and the smell of damp lingered in the air.

Mick stepped forward and opened one of the cells, stooping as he walked in. There was a small table and chair set against the wall.

"Here George, sit down there for a while. I've got to go over to the keg room, I'll be back in about an hour," he said.

The hinge on the top of the door made a springing sound when he left the cellar. I sat down. It was cold so I pulled up my hood and stared out the gate. Above my head there was a small round circle; it drew my attention away from the bars.

I crossed my legs, folded my arms, tipped my head back, and noticed a spider in its web. It ran towards the highest part of its citadel and waited to see if it would get any visitors that lacked judgment. But no one came, so it spun a line and hung down dangling in mid-air, only inches away from me.

"Hello there Mr Spider," I said, "No visitors today I see. Let's make a deal. You stay in your web and I'll stay in mine."

A wind blew in from the cage door, it made a haunting sound sending the small pieces of paper that were on the ground run for cover. The tiny spider set its eyes upon me, but it never spoke. It must have somehow picked up on what I was saying, because it climbed up the thin line back to its home, curled up into a ball and went to sleep.

The hinge on the door made that springing sound again. I jumped to my feet. A man in his late forties stood on the opposite side of the bars. He was dressed in a black jacket and grey pin-stripe trousers. His hair was cut tight and he wore a beard that was cut around his jaw-line.

"You must be George?" said the man in an upper class accent.

He placed his hand between the bars and we shook hands. It was a strong hand shake that was accompanied by a friendly smile.

"I am Mr Pat Burns, the assistant manager," he then added, walking into the cell.

He pulled over a few crates and sat down.

"Here Mr Burns, you sit here," I said pointing to the chair.

"Not at all, I am not an oul fella yet," he said, while rubbing his fist into his open hand.

We sat there for almost an hour talking, covering every subject known to man, and our hearts somehow bonded and a friendship was birthed.

"This place needs a good going over," he said. "But the only thing that can be done is to leave the cellar for now and concentrate on the boiler house."

He made a funny gesture with his mouth and we both burst out laughing. He stood to his feet and again shook my hand and said:"Yis are a bunch of cowboys. Right follow me Georgie Porgy and I will show you the boiler house."

The walls of the boiler house were coated in dust and dirt that had come with age. In the far corner there were sacks that were filled with old newspapers and a light timber tea-chest that had printed writing on the side. But to my good fortune it was very warm unlike the cellar.

Mr Burns walked over towards an old chair and table and tapped his foot against a small box that seemed to be fastened to the wall. It wouldn't open so he pressed down on it with an old spoon he had found. His eyes glistened when he finally opened it, and so did mine. He sat down slowly, and took from it, what must have been, two thousand pounds and an old book.

"Cowboys, Cowboys," I heard him say under his breath.

"George, call the porter down and tell him to bring a plastic bag with him."

"Yes, Mr Burns," I replied and left.

When I returned with the porter, Mr Burns placed the money and the old book into the bag and ordered the porter to bring it up to the head manager's office. It was discovered later that the money had been missing for years.

When they had left, I set about cleaning the old boiler house. Big Mick came back and stood at the door with two plates of hot food in his hands.

"Here George, Mag sent that down. I told her we would eat down here today. I'll bring yah up to the canteen when yah settle in."

"Nice one, Mick," I said as I sat down on the crate resting the plate on my lap and spooning it down as quickly as I could. I wanted to get back to cleaning the boiler house. Mick rose to his feet let out a large belch and said, "I'll be back in a while. Tomorrow I'll show yah the ropes."

"Ok Mick, see yah later."

No sooner had Mick left the room when I was up on my feet pulling at the boxes. I reached into the tea-chest and found an old Bible. I opened it. The pages were brown, the ink was faded and it smelled of must.

I glanced around the room and then began to read. I tucked it into my trousers and finished cleaning the room. When I had finished, I left the room and entered the cell, placing the Bible on the table. I glanced up again at the spider.

"Here I'll have to give you a name - Bilbo, yeah Bilbo that's your name Mr Spider."

My heart began to burn as my eyes pierced the pages.

"Here listen to this Bilbo, 'For God so loved the world, he gave his one and only Son, that whoever believes shall not perish but have eternal life'. That's you and me Bilbo, because we fit into the who-ever part."

"Will yah give us a hand with these, Georgie," Mick shouted

When I reached him he was pushing a line of empty kegs. So I pulled them along the corridor with him. It was a far cry from playing in front of 70,000 people, but I had bills to pay and a wife and baby to support.

Christmas after Christmas passed and another baby died. I felt a lot of compassion for Daniel when I watched him playing all alone. So I prayed in the cells a lot. Faith arose in my heart and I trusted that the Lord would visit us again.

On the 16th of February 1994, Nathan Lewis Fitzgerald was born into the world to the delight of us all.

"He'll be a warrior, Sandra he's a strong heart, I know it," I said.

When Sandra was pregnant with Nathan, she experienced difficulties. The doctors told us that there wasn't much hope. At the time we had lost three children. But I prayed to Jesus. And one day met a man of faith, by the name of Steven Monse. He prayed on the streets of Finglas, pleading the blood of Jesus over the unborn child and rested his hand on my shoulder and said "No weapon formed against you shall prosper." And low and behold, Nathan was born weighing 9lbs.

♪

One dull day, I noticed a tiny black dot on the table. It was Bilbo, he had gone asleep but he wasn't going to wake up anymore. A voice called me, it came from behind. I turned around just as I reached the end of the narrow passageway and saw that it was the gentleman himself Mr Burns.

"George they are out of wine in the Tea Rooms. Will you go and get some up for them, I'll be back in a minute," he said and then left.

The hotel had changed hands. The band U2 had bought it, in partnership with Harry Crosby.

As I reached the ground floor, I bumped into Louis Walsh. He was standing with Ronan Keating. We exchanged a few words and I left.

I spotted Andrea Corr; she seemed to be waiting on someone. I rushed down the steps and shared a few new ideas I had. She hadn't a clue who I was, but she was kind enough to listen.

When I entered the Tea Rooms, Gavin Friday was there, sitting beside Naomi Campbell. He called me, so I went over, and then he introduced me to the beautiful lady. She shook my hand and talked a bit, and as the conversation was moving, I turned my head slightly and caught sight of Rizzo heading into the bar. And as luck would have it, the barman asked me if I could empty the bottle bin. I said goodbye and walked into the bar full of rage.

There they all were, and here I was, emptying bins. And the man that had a major part to play in destroying our band was sitting right beside the bin I was about to empty.

Louis Walsh, Naomi Campbell, Gavin Friday, Andréa Corr, and now Rizzo, who could have imagined it. I nodded to him and smiled. I actually asked after him. He looked at me with a silent stare and for a moment I thought that he might ask if I would clean his shoes, well after all I was wearing an apron.

"See yah Rizzo," I said as I arched my back and pushed the bin out of the bar. When I got down to the cellar, I exploded. I kicked the wall and hurt my foot. Mick was the first to speak

"Georgie your pride is hurt that's all."

"That's great, if you're a poet, but I am afraid I don't feel very poetic today," I said as I sat and smoked twenty cigarettes and drank a pot of coffee.

"Yis bunch of cowboys," Mr Burns said when he walked back in.

"Here, you have a word with him. I've got to go over to the cold room anyway," Mick said.

Mr Burns listened as I poured out my complaint, waited until I finished and then he said: "George, I once knew a young mother who was told by the doctors that her days were numbered. And on the day I visited her, I found her in joyful spirits. I pushed her in a wheelchair down along the corridor of the hospital, she asked me to stop, so I did. And then she remarked on how beautiful the trees were, the birds and the different shades of greens that ran between the grass and the leaves.

"Oh yes," she said, "This is a wonderful day."

When I was about to leave, I asked her how she would spend her evening. She said, "By counting the stars, marvelling at the sky and feeling the wonderment of life, but best of all, I get to see the faces of people, wonderful people, just like you."

She tipped my hand and then said, "Thank you for sharing this wonderful day with me, because when I sleep tonight, I might not wake again, but I thank God for every moment of every day now."

"Georgie, she never did wake up again."

He rose off his seat and tipped my shoulder. I couldn't look up. The tears filled my eyes, because I knew the identity of the woman - it was his wife.

"You're a rough diamond Georgie, don't let little things bother you anymore."

I jumped up, brushed away the tears and we embraced.

"Sorry for yah troubles, Mr Burns."

"Sure the good Lord said that he would carry them for me Georgie."

"Mr Burns," I shouted, "Why do they call the Lord the son of David?"

"Because he wasn't ashamed to be identified with us," he said walking out the door.

When Mr Burns was gone, I pondered on all the things he told me. I was very happy about God and felt I loved him so I talked to him in the way the teacher told me to and I asked him to close his eyes while I go up and give Rizzo a box. But I knew that wasn't God's way so I kneeled in the cell and prayed. "Thank you Lord for Mr Burns and Mick, sorry for having pride, and I forgive Rizzo."

♪

We started a new band called Joseph. Joe, Pat, Paulo, and myself.

At the time we all had become very influenced by two books, 'The Cross and the Switchblade,' and 'Run Run Baby.'

Both books told the story of David Wilkerson, and Nicky Cruz. The books were first published around 1958 and to-date they have sold over thirty-five million copies world-wide.

Nicky was the head of the infamous New York gang called the Mau-Maus but after he had an encounter with the skinny preacher David Wilkerson, he became converted to Christ.

Joe had an idea, he wanted to record an album based on the books. But the problem was money so we started playing small venues until we reached the National Stadium and would you believe the guest speaker that night was Nicky Cruz. We got to sit and talk to him for a while and he invited us over to the States.

The band reached the finals of the Coca Cola awards hosted by Dave Fanning. It was ironic, because the first TV shows we did as 'The D11Runners' were also hosted by Dave. Eamon Carr ran a piece in the Evening Herald the following week.

In order to generate cash, Joe flew out to Los Angles. He was supposed to be meeting up with a Mexican named Art. Art was at one time the most wanted man the United States of America. He served ten years on death row in the infamous San Quentin prison. But he got the sentence overturned and he came out, robbed the Mafia and ran. But while he was locked up again he got converted and it changed his whole life. But Joe missed Art, he had just gone to England. Joe wasn't alone as Sonny was with him. Sonny had been put in contact with Peter Traynor. And in many ways that says it all.

Peter carried the cross into the world of the gun and reached not only Sonny, but Little Bo. When the time was right he arranged for them to be flown away to centres in Scotland and Wales. When they landed on the shores of Ireland a year or so later they never went back to crime or took drugs again.

Joe and Sonny flew home, then Joe was off to England to do TV shows. The rest of us flew to Scotland where we met up and played a series of dates. When we arrived home Joe was put in contact with Billy Farrell. He had produced The Corrs album and also Westlife. Now all we needed was about twenty grand.

Art flew to Dublin and spoke at a convention, we got to talk with him. Sonny showed him around the city for about a week while we sat and listened to a man by the name of Packy Hamilton. He had served ten years in H-Block, but like Art he was also dramatically saved. He came to my home and talked about faith and hope and told us to be strong and remain faithful. I was amazed at these men and prayed that God would do the same for us.

♪

Security guards were dressed in light jackets filled the streets outside the hotel. I pushed the bar and opened the door of The Kitchen night club, and glanced across the busy streets.

The sun was hot and the air was heavy. I noticed Bono and the Edge walking towards me. They nodded as they went past, so I nodded back, while I closed the door behind me. They stopped just in front of the main door and talked with one of the manageresses, Miss Ariane.

After a few minutes she left them and began walking in my direction looking purposeful and determined. She placed her finger on her lips, commanding the little hummingbirds that had gathered outside to be quiet. The phone she was carrying rang, she lifted it to her ear, and talked and walked while the jacket of her trouser suit blew in the light breeze.

A limousine pulled up and a chauffeur got out. The window rolled down and Miss Ariane spoke to one of the world's most famous actors. A minute or two later, he stepped out of the car and followed Bono and the Edge up the stairs of the hotel. She stepped cautiously past a crowd of onlookers and then landed within inches of me.

"You must be George," she said as I studied her. She was very young with eyes that were sharp, perfect hair style and a strong

French accent, but her words were as clear as any English teacher. She stared at me for a moment. I glanced down as if I was having a conversation with my shoe.

"Yeah that's me," I said as I raised my head.

"Good George, I have news for you. Your days in the cellar are over, follow me," she then said as she walked off.

"Miss Ariane, will I get my gear from the cellar?" I shouted from behind.

"Call me Ariane," she whispered with a smile.

Before I could second-guess her she opened the door of the stores and led me in. Over at the far wall there was a large table and chair, a phone, and on the table was a blue Bible.

"We do our homework," she said faintly.

"Thank you."

"Right George, tell me about yourself," she said as she pulled a chair over.

I started off with Ballymun, Finglas, the boxing, and the band.

"That's an amazing story, did you ever think of writing it down?"

Before I could answer the buzzer went, the door opened and Dave Dowling walked in and a friendship began between the three of us that still continues to this day.

Ariane asked me to recite my story to Dave so I did.

"He should write that down, don't you think Dave?"

"Yeah, it would make for an interesting read."

"Have you got a title?" Dave asked. I paused for a moment and then said, "Yeah, I'd call it 'Somebody Up There Likes Me Too'."

A few minutes later Dave left. The stores fell silent. Ariane asked me a question.

"Are you happy here?"

"It's ok."

"If you have a gift and I think you have, because you can demand people's attention with your words. And if so, write it down don't waste your gift."

"I will one day."

"No George, as you Irish say, strike while the iron's hot," she said closing the door.

Joe flew over to London and did a showcase in a football stadium. When he arrived home we were interviewed by Mark Cassidy on TV3 and then we met Maire Brennan. She is a very genuine woman and full of humility. She helped the band and she asked me if I would plaster her new studio. I said yes. It was just after she won the Grammie. We talked about her band Clannad and films and music.

But all the years striving were beginning to catch up on me. I just didn't want to do it anymore. The focus and passion were gone. So I rang Joe and told him. I left the hotel and went back plastering. In 2002, I bought a new home, a semi-detached show house in Dublin 15.

I walked around the roof of the flats I was working on. I picked up the newspaper and saw that Benny and Paddy the Lip made the headlines. Both of them had been shot dead. Anto overdosed shortly before and died at thirty two years of age. I stared across the roof top. What was it all about? A lot of the kids I'd grown up were dead. Joe counted the names and came up with one hundred and forty kids from the neighbourhood - dead. It was something I'd thought about a lot. I thought of the young faces. What went wrong? I thought.

"What's the story, Georgie? The lads are all looking for yah. They want yah to tell one of your stories."

"Not today Barry McGuinness, not today. I've had enough of

stories for one day."

"What's wrong?"

"Nothing, I'm just tired that's all."

"Did yah start to write your book yet?"

"No Barry, haven't got the time."

"Well Georgie, if I was you I'd give it a go. What have yah got to lose? The plastering will always be here."

"Yeah," I said, "Come on let's get back to work."

But it wasn't until one Sunday I was listening to the world famous motivational speaker, T D Jakes. He pointed out and said, "God has put it into the heart of a man out there to write a book."

Shortly after I started writing, I was walking up along the stairwell of the flats and received sharp pains in my chest. The doctor told me that there was a possibility that I had suffered two heart attacks. It turned out to be a chest infection. That progressed to a lung infection. I kept writing. The cough didn't go away. I was beginning to look sick. I went back to the doctor and he told me I was borderline pneumonia, chronic bronchitis, and my air waves were nearly closed. "If you would have left it until Monday you could have been dead."

I sat on his bed, my face stuck to a ventilator telling him about the book. I kept writing while growing weaker. But I felt encouraged when I'd listen to TD Jakes, Joyce Myers. It was like God sent word through, "No weapon formed against you shall prosper."

Finally on New Years Eve 2003, I was sent to the hospital. I had some x-rays taken and the doctor told me that there was a small possibility that I had lung cancer. But my doctor refuted that report. I was sent for more x-rays.

I was told to ring on Friday. I got a phone call. It was my doctor.

"George."

"Yes, doctor."

"I have great news, your lungs are clear. You don't have cancer."

I walked upstairs and fell down on the bed and thanked God. Three days later, I went for an interview for a job doing Security. My job entailed sitting in a box and keeping an eye on cars.

So this is where this story ends. I am sitting in a box on South William Street. I put pen to paper and wrote my story, worrying about grammar, while trying to construct a sentence and form a paragraph. But I kept going. I left school at fifteen years of age. I never attended a writers' workshop, or an English class. I never studied editing; I hardly ever read a book.

On the 5th of Feb, 2005, the day of my ma's birthday, I was finished. I walked out into the street and looked up to heaven as I rubbed my dog's head. He's a lovely white boxer, called Max. And I said, "Here Max, Rocky was right. Somebody up there likes me too."

What was it like for me to write this book? Well let me take you on one last journey, let me take you by the hand and show you what I saw.

I am climbing a mountain. I remember Davy's words, "I'll be standing on the tallest mountain you ever did see with my arm stretched out, waiting for an eagle to land."

I reached the peak only to find a larger mountain above me. When I was too tired to go on I'd rest on the rocks while being visited by imaginary friends, one called Hopeful, the other Encouragement. I asked Hopeful, why I didn't find friends while climbing the mountain?

"Because then you would not have found Character," he replied.

"Now wait here." I waited and waited until I understood that Hopeful lived inside of me. I reached the top, looked over the edge and saw men starting to climb, shouting to one another, "Keep to the narrow path." Then a large eagle stood beside me. He had the face of a man and spoke like a lion. "I am Wisdom, I journeyed with you. There is someone over there who wants to talk to you." I looked across the mountain in the distance. I saw a man way off holding his arm stretched out.

"Is that you Davy?" I roared.

"No."

"Who are you?"

"I am the Son of David."

I sat down and pondered, "It was you Lord all along, in every voice, in ever finger that pointed the way, from the dunce's corner, to the mountain top." I stood up.

"The Lord shouted, "Start flapping your wings George."

"Why Lord?"

He roared in a loud voice, "Because an eagle is about to fly...."